INSTANT BUSINESS LETTER KIT

KIT

Third Edition

INSTANT BUSINESS LETTER KIT

HOW TO WRITE BUSINESS LETTERS THAT GET THE JOB DONE
THIRD EDITION

By Shaun Fawcett, M.B.A.

"How-To" Tips & Tricks Style Guide
plus
129 Fully-Formatted Real-Life Templates!

BUSINESS LETTERS: for large, medium, small, and home business

SPECIAL BONUS CHAPTER: *"Writing Business Reports"*

National Library of Canada Cataloguing in Publication Data

Fawcett, Shaun, 1949-
Instant business letter kit : how to write business letters
that get the job done / Shaun Fawcett – 3rd ed.

Includes bibliographical references.
Issued also in electronic format.

ISBN 978-0-9812898-8-5

1. Letter Writing. 2. Commercial correspondence. I. Title.
HF5726.F388 2013   808'.06665   C2013-900498-X

Final Draft Publications
911-400 rue de l'Inspecteur
Montreal QC, Canada H3C 4A8

http://www.WritingHelpTools.com

TABLE OF CONTENTS

Special Note Re: Hyperlinks

Because this book was first created and published online as a digital download e-book with "live" clickable hyperlinks throughout, those same links have been displayed in their entirety in this printed version for your information and use. Even though the links are not clickable in this paperback version of the book, they still provide pertinent website URL addresses that you can type into your Internet browser should you want to explore online for further information.

The hyperlinks are easily identifiable because they are <u>underlined</u> just as they would be on a website or in an e-book.

Dedication

The Third Edition of this e-book is dedicated to the thousands of people worldwide who have showed their trust in me over the years by purchasing the previous versions of this book, as well as my other writing help books and e-books. I thank them for their support and encouragement.

PREFACE TO SPECIAL PRINT EDITION

The previous version of *Instant Business Letter Kit (Second Edition)* was published both as an e-book and in paperback form in 2006. As such, it has been available through traditional booksellers and distributors, in both forms, since that time.

It has also been available as a digital download e-book from the dedicated website: http://www.instantbusinessletterkit.com

From the moment that website went "live" the e-book has sold very well because buyers were able to purchase and download it immediately to their computer hard drive.

Nevertheless, I realized from the beginning that no matter how much I publicized that website, many people in need of business letter writing help and information would never become aware of it. I also knew that a certain group of people would prefer a standard printed paper book, over the e-book version.

So I decided to also use alternative, more conventional distribution channels.

Consequently, this particular version is a special one that is being made available through more traditional book marketing channels. So, if you are reading this paperback version, it should be because you purchased it through a large traditional book distribution company such as amazon.com, barnesandnoble.com, or other similar standard book retailers.

Get Your Downloadable Templates

There is one key difference between this book that you purchased through a book distributor or retailer and that which you would have received had you purchased and downloaded the e-book version from my website.

Website purchasers can instantly download the Bonus Templates (MS-Word format) straight to their computer at the time of purchase. However, for technical reasons, that is not possible when purchasing the book in printed form through distributors such as amazon.com and conventional bookstores.

But, since the templates are an integral part of the Kit, I wanted to make sure that owners of the printed book also have access to them.

To receive your FREE copy of the Bonus Templates file, please send an e-mail with the required "proof of purchase" information to the following address:
mailto:templates85@instantbusinessletterkit.com

In that e-mail you MUST include the following information:
Your full name; full telephone number; your primary e-mail address; and the date of purchase. Also indicate which business you purchased the Kit from, and include the Order Number or Transaction Number that you were given at the time of purchase. (If it's convenient you can just forward your online invoice or receipt to me).

Once I have received your e-mail and verified your purchase, I will Reply to you with the Bonus Templates as an attachment to the e-mail. Normally, you should receive that file within a few hours of making your request -- 24 hours at the most.

This Book Has Two Parts

As explained above, when the e-book is sold from my website it comes in two downloadable parts as follows:

1. Instant Business Letter Kit (288 page pdf e-book)

2. Bonus Templates (202 page MS-Word doc)

In total, you get a two-part book of almost 500 pages.

As stated above, the downloadable Bonus Templates file may be ordered for Free by e-mail at the following address:
mailto:templates85@instantbusinessletterkit.com

REMEMBER, when requesting your downloadable Bonus Templates make sure you include the following information in your e-mail:

Your full name, full telephone number, your primary e-mail address, and the date of purchase. Please indicate which business you purchased the Kit from, and include the Order Number or Transaction Number that you were given at the time of purchase.

INTRODUCTION

REVISED EDITION NOTES

The first version of *Instant Business Letter Kit* was published as an e-book in the summer of 2002, followed by a Revised Edition in 2006. Both editions were offered as a digital download e-book from a website, as well as through retailers that offer digital downloads of PDF e-books.

Since 2006, the *Revised Edition* of the Kit has also been widely available in printed paperback form via amazon.com and other print distributors.

The main reason why I decided to release a *Third Edition* at this time was to add some additional real-life letter templates that I have developed over the past few years – 29 new ones. Otherwise the style guide content has changed very little, aside from minor tweaks and updates here and there. Nothing major though, beyond the addition of the new templates.

There are a few reasons why I decided to create *Instant Business Letter Kit* in the first place. First and foremost, I believed (and continue to believe) that there is a serious need for a comprehensive business letter style guide that is based on true <u>real-life templates</u>.

This conclusion is based on extensive research that I have done into business letter writing products currently on the market, both online and offline. The fact is, I have found that the vast majority of business letter writing products out there are based on the old model of "copying and pasting" generic "dumbed-down" blocks of text.

Those products have NO style guide, NO formatting guidelines, and NO resource links – just blocks of generic text.

In almost all cases, the vendors of those products refer to their blocks of generic texts as "templates" -- but that's NOT what they really are. In reality, a block of generic text does NOT make a true template -- simply supplying blocks of copy-and-paste text is NOT providing actual real-life templates.

In my mind, **a true business letter template** is a fully-formatted, properly laid out letter that gives the user everything they need to know to be able to create a final product including: address block, opening salutation, complete real-life body text, and closing signature block – all in the context of an actual real-life situation.

The fact is that I have not been able to find EVEN ONE of these so-called business letter writing products, online or offline, that provides complete fully-formatted real-life templates -- as I've described them in the previous paragraph. The ONLY product that I know of that offers true real-life templates is *Instant Business Letter Kit*. Really.

In short, I believe that a product based on fully-formatted real-life templates is essential for anyone who wants to produce professional quality business letters.

The main reason why I decided to issue a revised *Third Edition* of *Instant Business Letter Kit* was to provide additional letter templates that I have developed for various situations over the past few years, since the 2006 *Second Edition*.

In total, I have added 29 new letter templates. Of course, these are all fully formatted, full-length, real-life templates that deal with actual business situations.

I also took the opportunity to review the style guide part of the Kit – the first 70 pages or so – and made some minor revisions and additions. I also reviewed and updated the online resource links for both "Business Letter How-To Resources" and "Business Letter Services and Tools". In addition, the keyword index has been updated to reflect the latest content and letter templates.

I have no doubt whatsoever, that this *Third Edition* of *Instant Business Letter Kit* is the most complete, comprehensive, and practical resource that you will find anywhere on the subject of how-to write professional quality business letters based on real-life business situations.

BACKGROUND

My name is Shaun Fawcett. I am a Canadian-based writer, publisher, business consultant, and journalist. Over the past 30 years I have worked in a variety of professional capacities in both the private and public sectors. I earned my M.B.A. in 1996 through the University of Ottawa's Executive MBA Program. Online since 1993, I am Webmaster of numerous writing related websites. Below is a summary of my experiences which I believe qualify me to write this business letter writing kit.

In 2001 I set up my first writing help website, www.WritingHelpCentral.com. My idea at the time was to create a small portal site that offered free writing help content and provided links to the writing related products of others.

Since then, that WritingHelpCentral website has grown significantly. As I write this, that site contains almost 400 pages and over 300,000 words of free writing-help-related content covering such topics as: letter writing, resume/c.v. writing, essay writing, book writing, business writing, copy writing, and much more.

By 2013 that website was receiving an average of over 6,000 unique visitors from more than 200 countries, each and every day. In fact, on some peak week days, the total unique visitor count currently exceeds 8,000 people from all around the world!

Now, with almost 2.0 million unique visitors per year, WritingHelpCentral is among the top ten or so "writing help" destinations on the entire Internet. And, its sister site, www.WritingHelpTools.com isn't far behind.

I am also the author of a popular e-mail writing help course called "Tips and Trick For Writing Success". As of early 2013, more than 100,000 people in over 210 countries had participated in that course, and I receive positive testimonials from participants on a regular basis.

In addition to that course, I offer a number of other writing-related courses from my various Websites. You can sign up for any or all of these courses at: http://writinghelptools.com/all-courses.html

One advantage of operating popular destination websites like I do is that they provide one with the perfect research and development "laboratory" in which to find out what people in a particular niche are REALLY looking for.

For example, because my Writing Help Central website has attracted literally millions of people with letter writing information needs over the past decade, I have been able to study EXACTLY what these visitors are really looking for in the way of letter writing help and information.

As a result, I am willing to bet that I am the top authority on the entire Internet when it comes to knowing EXACTLY what letter writing help most people are actually searching for online. That includes business letter writing needs.

In parallel with my writing help content websites, I maintain a writing help blog called "The Write Place" where I post writing-related articles and info once or twice a month. You can check out my writing help blog at:
http://writinghelptools.com/blog/

WHY I WROTE THIS BOOK

Since 2001 I have written a series of writing help toolkit e-books/books designed to cater to the needs of people looking for letter writing help. In addition to InstantBusinessLetterKit.com, here are the others:

Instant Recommendation Letter Kit
http://instantrecommendationletterkit.com

Instant Letter Writing Kit
http://instantletterwritingkit.com

Instant Resignation Letter Kit
http://instantresignationletterkit.com

Instant Home Writing Kit
http://instanthomewritingkit.com

As the above titles clearly indicate, these toolkits are highly targeted to address very specific letter writing needs. I developed these particular products because my research indicated that help with writing these specific types of letters was much in demand.

In addition to the development of the above-listed publications based on the needs of visitors to my websites, my research also showed that more than 50% of people looking for letter writing help on my websites were looking for help with "business letters".

However, when I looked further into that I realized that there was a lot of confusion among folks as to exactly what they meant by "business letter" as opposed to such letters as: employee letters, sales letters, reference letters, application letters, etc.

So, it was all of that interest in the subject of "business letters" in general -- coupled with the apparent confusion that seemed to surround the topic -- that prompted me to write the first version of *Instant Business Letter Kit* back in 2002.

Now, after more than a decade observing and studying the letter writing help needs of all of my visitors who search for such information, I am in the unique position of being able to state unequivocally which specific business letters are most often searched for, and in what order of priority.

Instant Business Letter Kit is another highly focused book, in the same way as the the other letter writing toolkits cited on the previous page. It focuses on the development and writing of the various types of "business letters" which I have divided into two broad categories; for reasons which I'll explain later:

1. **Business-to-Business letters** (i.e. other businesses, internal business)

2. **Business-to-Customer letters** (i.e. consumers, general public)

Again, the idea for this particular book grew directly out of observing visitor behavior and preferences at my writing help website:
http://www.writinghelp-central.com.

As a result, I concluded that there was a definite need for a practical quick reference "business letter kit" combined with "real-life" sample templates.

Accordingly, *Instant Business Letter Kit* was conceived and designed as a quick-reference guide for business, home, and home-business writing, focused on simplifying the often difficult and delicate task of writing the various types of business letters. Most importantly, it is a practical hands-on "toolkit" that people can use whenever they have to write a business letter of any kind.

Using the fully-formatted "real-life templates" included with the Kit, you will never again have to start writing a business letter from a blank page or screen. You can work directly from the real-life templates that you can download straight into your word-processing program (MS-Word compatible).

Bottom line: If you ever need to write ANY type of business letter, this Kit will definitely simplify your life.

WHAT THIS WRITING KIT INCLUDES

This business letter-writing toolkit is much more than just a bunch of templates quickly thrown together, as is often the case with many manuals of this type.

As mentioned earlier, the contents of this Kit is the result of over ten (10) years of research into the "writing help needs" of the average Web surfer looking for letter-writing help.

In fact, the Kit is a complete and comprehensive business letter-writing style guide that contains more than 127 fully-formatted real-life templates, and is comprised of **three major components.**

Component number ONE is a letter-writing "how-to" style guide combined with the fully-formatted real-life sample letters.

Component number TWO is a set of fully-formatted real-life letter templates that can be downloaded straight into a standard word processing program such as MS-Word.

Component number THREE is comprised of lists of fully-researched online resources that focus on advice, information, and tools related to business-letter writing.

Style Guide

The style guide part of the Kit contains over 67 pages of business letter-writing "how-to" information including letter-writing tips, strategies and pointers, as well as letter formatting guidelines for writing all types of business letters.

For the First Revised Edition, I added a chapter to the style guide section that describes a step-by-step foolproof method for quickly and easily using a real-life letter template to develop your own customized business letter. This proprietary **Template Adaptation Method**[TM] is a powerful technique that you can use for ANY business letter situation.

More than 127 fully-formatted real-life sample letters are also included to graphically demonstrate how to write each letter-type and to show you what the final product should look like. These are REAL letters -- NOT your typical fill-in-the-blank, cut-and-paste jobs that proliferate the Internet.

Templates

For each of the 127-plus sample letters, a fully formatted real-life template is provided in a form that can be downloaded straight into your word processor. The templates have been divided into two overall groups as follows:

1. Business-to-business letters.
2. Business-to-customer letters.

Important Note

People who purchase this Kit as an e-book directly from my website receive the templates file as a download at the time of purchase. Those who buy the Kit through book retailers such as amazon.com, barnesandnoble.com and regular booksellers have the option to request that the templates file be sent to them by e-mail. The information for doing this is available in the Special Preface at the beginning of this book.

Business Letter Resources

In addition to the above, the Kit also includes researched letter-writing resources:

1. **Top 20 Business Letter Writing Resource Websites** - My own exclusive fully-researched list of websites that offer business letter writing advice and information.

2. **Top Business Letter Writing References** - My personal "desert island list" list of recommended writing reference texts.

Instant Business Letter Kit also includes a detailed Table of Contents and a fully cross-referenced Keyword Index for quick and easy reference.

Bonus Chapter - Business Report Writing

This book also includes a Bonus Chapter on the subject of Writing Business Reports of all types. In that chapter I include my personal tips and techniques that I have learned over 30 years experience writing scores of business reports of just about every type.

The chapter includes Table of Contents outlines for five major report types: Business Proposal, Corporate Profile, Strategic Plan, Project Review, and Business Plan.

The Bonus Chapter also includes my proprietary Universal Process Flow Diagram^{TM} (UPFD) which can be used to improve and add credibility to ANY type of report that you need to write.

WHO THIS BOOK IS FOR

This Kit was written to help ANYONE who needs to write business letters for any type of business or personal situation for which a business letter is appropriate.

Whether you work for a large corporation, operate your own small to medium business, or you run a home-based business, the letters in this Kit will help you. The size of the operation isn't really a determining factor when it comes to communicating via business letters. Business letter situations are essentially generic and will use the same type of letter and approach to writing, regardless of the size of the business sending it.

As stated earlier, this book contains over 127 real-life sample templates of the most requested business letters at my writing help websites. In fact, I know that these sample templates cover more than 99% of ALL business letters you will ever need to write.

In fact, I am willing to back up that last statement with the following guarantee:

If you find a case for which you need a business letter, and not one of the templates in the Kit can be easily adapted to meet your need, let me know. **If I agree that there is no appropriate template in the Kit that you can use, I'll write the letter for you!**

Now, how's that for a guarantee!

DON'T SKIP THE FIRST 67 PAGES!

I know from experience that the initial inclination of many people buying this Kit will be to jump straight into the sample templates without even pausing to look at the advice, tips, pointers and other information at the beginning of this Kit.

BE WARNED: If you skip the first 67 pages of this book you will be missing lots of valuable/useful information that you won't find anywhere else!

In fact, if you ignore that style guide information you will be missing out on the bulk of unique information that differentiates this book from those others that just provide blocks of cut-and-paste generic text. (That is, aside from the real-life templates that are included here, of course).

It will be well worth a few minutes of your time to review the writing style information in the first part of this Kit. The information included in the "style guide" part of the Kit is based on over 30 years of experience writing thousands of business and professional letters. So, don't miss it!

Whatever you do, **DO NOT MISS the section on "Use The Template Adaptation Method" (see pg. 63).** That technique alone is well worth the price of this Kit.

WHAT THIS MANUAL COVERS

This manual covers a wide variety of business letters. Although -- somewhat surprisingly -- the term "business letters" often confuses people.

This point was confirmed when I conducted my research for this guide. As I browsed the bookshelves and websites, it quickly became clear that there is no widely accepted definition as to "exactly" what a business letter actually is, when compared with, say, a personal letter, or an employee letter, for example.

Once I started looking into it more closely, it wasn't that hard to understand why there was so much confusion about business letters. It's not always as straightforward as it might seem at first glance.

For example; what if the letter involves personal business? Do you classify it as personal or business? Is a "letter of introduction" a business letter or a personal letter? How about a "cover letter"? Clearly, a "resume cover letter" is a personal letter. But then there are "business cover letters" too. A cover letter for a report that is being sent from one company to another is one example.

There are many other examples of this kind of confusion as to what exactly constitutes a business letter, and what doesn't.

A good way to confirm this is to go to your local bookstore and check out the business books section. You might find half a dozen different books about writing business letters. Look at the Table of Contents in a few of these. See if you can find a common thread of logic as to what classifies as a "business letter" and what doesn't. Good luck!

So, for reasons of clarity, I have developed my own business letter definition and classification system for this guide.

Don't get me wrong. I'm not trying to re-invent the wheel here. Let's just say that the wheel is already rotating but it could be working a little better. I'm simply going to tighten it up, add some oil, and take the wobble out.

Two Broad Categories of Business Letters

I believe that the defining element that determines whether a letter is a business letter, or not, is the specific "context" within which it is written.

I also believe that business letters can be divided into two broad categories, based on the intended recipient. These two recipient groups are: 1.) businesses, and 2.) customers or consumers.

Accordingly, the letters in this manual are divided into two broad categories based on intended recipient: 1.) business-to-business, and 2.) business-to-customer.

Both of these categories are further subdivided into logical groups based on the specific purpose of the individual letter.

To illustrate, let's go back to one of the examples cited above – letter of introduction. In the business-to-business category, there will be an introduction letter specific to that grouping. On the other hand, there will be a different type of letter of introduction in the business-to-customer category.

Generally speaking, purely "personal letters" are not included in this guide.

For example, "resume cover letters" are NOT included here because they are simply not defined as business letters. They are a type of personal or employment-related letter. You will find these letters in their proper context - a resume writing guide.

On the other hand, a "cover letter" for a report is included as a standard business-to-business letter.

Business-to-Business Letters

These are defined as typical letters that businesses send to one another in "normal" business situations ("normal" in the sense of "typical").

By "business" I mean any kind of enterprise, for-profit or non-profit, which activities focus on the creation and/or delivery of a good or service.

For the purposes of this guide I am referring to any size or type of business enterprise including small, medium, large, and home business. This definition also includes institutional enterprises such as governments and not-for-profit agencies.

Typical business-to-business letters include: price quotations, meeting confirmations, order confirmations, joint venture proposals, financial letters, project status reports, news releases, invitations to participate, etc.

Also covered in the business-to-business category are some types of typical "internal" correspondence such as the inter-office memorandum and employee letters.

A more detailed discussion of business-to-business letters can be found on page 30.

Business-to-Customer Letters

Business-to-customer letters are defined as typical letters that businesses send to their customers under normal operating circumstances.

When I refer to "customers" here, it is mostly in the sense of the individual consumer. Business letters addressed to individual customers are usually different in approach and content from business-to-business letters.

Typical business-to-customer letters include: sales letters, introduction letters, collection letters, letters of apology, thank you letters, responses to complaints, credit acceptance/refusal letters, service follow-up letters, order acknowledgement letters, collection letters, announcement letters, etc.

A more detailed discussion of business-to-customer letters can be found on page 31.

Letters NOT Included In This Guide

As mentioned above, there are a number of letter types that are NOT included in this manual because they are not actually "business letters" but are more personal and home related letters.

Letters of this nature that are NOT included in this manual include: resume cover letters, letters of recommendation, character and job reference letters, letters to landlords, complaint letters, personal thank you letters, resignation letters, job inquiry letters, and other letters of a personal nature such as letters of apology, congratulations, invitation, and condolence, among others.

These types of personal letters that don't fall into the business category can be found in the appropriate category in a number of my other Writing Guides at: http://www.WritingHelpTools.com

Writing Business Reports

As mentioned earlier, in addition to the various types of business letters, I have also included a **Bonus Chapter on *"Writing Business Reports"*.**

In this chapter I share many of the tips, tricks and techniques that I have learned over the years while writing scores of business reports of just about every type imaginable. Of course, it only makes sense to also include such a chapter in this guide since the focus here is on business writing (see pg. 241).

Business Writing References

I have included a section that contains a list of what I consider to be the top reference and style guides available for both writing in general and business writing in particular.

This section includes some 15 to 20 publication titles and links should one need to consult other references to assist with their business writing. (see pg. 261).

Online Resource Links

This guide also contains a section of fully-researched links to online writing resources related to the writing of business letters.

There are literally tens of thousands of resources on the Internet related to the writing of business letters. To save you the time and trouble of trying to sift your way through all of that information, I have included a section in this guide with links to what I consider the **Top 20 online resources** related to the writing of business letters. (see pg. 265).

Theses links are divided into two groups: how-to links and writing services and tools.

REAL-LIFE TEMPLATES FOR SUCCESS

Before getting into the specifics of business letters, I believe it is important to discuss the presentation of the business letters that are included later in this guide. After all, it's likely that one or more of the letter templates included here will have significant influence on what you send out in the mail to a business or customer.

All of the sample templates for the various types of business letters contained in this Kit are presented in a format that I call "fully-formatted real-life templates". In fact, it is these real-life downloadable templates which make all of my writing kits unique. These are also what my customers have told me they love about my writing kits.

Real-life templates are ACTUAL letters written for - yes, you guessed it - "real-life" situations. ALL of the letters in this Kit were written for real-life situations.

I am convinced that real-life templates are by far the most useful tools for people when they need to draft any kind of document. These templates are a quantum leap beyond the traditional one or two line "fill-in-the-blank" cut-and-paste templates.

The remainder of this section is an expanded and updated version of an article I first published a few years ago titled *"Use Real-Life Templates For Writing Success"*. It has since been published in various eZines and posted on numerous websites across the Internet.

"USE REAL-LIFE TEMPLATES FOR WRITING SUCCESS"

At some point, most of us have used what are commonly called "fill-in-the-blank" writing templates. It might have been to write a letter, format an essay, compose a report, or set up a resume.

What I'm talking about here are those form letter templates that you see in text books and work books with the blank lines and spaces where you're supposed to fill in the appropriate words.

Fill-In-The-Blank Template - Sample

For example, in the case of a letter to an employee, a typical "fill-in-the-blank" template would look something like this:

Dear [NAME OF RECIPIENT]:

This is to advise you that your probation period in the position [POSITION NAME] expired on [DATE].

The [NAME OF REVIEW COMMITTEE] met on [DATE OF MEETING] and determined that your probationary review period was successful and that you should be immediately appointed to [NAME OF POSITION] [NAME OF ORGANIZATIONAL UNIT].

Accordingly, this is to inform you that effective [DATE OF APPOINTMENT] you are officially appointed to the position of [NAME OF POSITION] for an initial period of [NUMBER OF YEARS/MONTHS]. Terms and conditions of your employment are covered by [OFFICIAL CONTRACT NAME/NUMBER].

Would you please report as soon as possible to [NAME OF OFFICIAL], [TITLE OF OFFICIAL] in the [OFFICIAL NAME OF HR GROUP] so that the details of your appointment may be properly documented.

Congratulations [NAME OF APPOINTEE]. All of us at [COMPANY OR ORGANIZATION NAME] look forward to working with you in the future.

Sincerely,

[NAME OF ORIGINATOR]
[TITLE OF ORIGINATOR]

Although this "fill-in-the-blank" approach can work, it has a number of drawbacks:

Disadvantages Of Fill-In-The-Blank Templates

- Because of their generic nature, they tend to generalize so much that they resemble a computer-generated form letter.

- They don't provide specific information on how a professional would properly fill in the required information [i.e. BLANK FIELDS].

- The content is typically watered-down using generic terms in order to try and cover every possible situation.

- They don't provide mental stimulation or show how a professional might word the letter in a specific real-life context.

- They are difficult to work with and virtually useless for 98% of real-life situations, since they lack real-life content.

Real-Life Letter Template - Sample

On the other hand, here's what a "real-life template" would look like for the same situation covered above:

Dear Jessica:

This is to advise you that your probation period in the position Customer Service Agent (Temporary) expired on November 30, 20xx.

The Staffing Review Committee met late last week and determined that your probationary review period was successful and that you should be appointed immediately as Customer Service Agent (Ongoing).

Accordingly, this is to inform you that effective December 1, 20xx, you are officially appointed to the position of Customer Service Agent in the Customer Support Group. The initial appointment will be for a period of 36 months. Terms and conditions of your employment are covered by the Customer Service Group Employment Agreement.

Would you please report as soon as possible to Jim Jackson, Chief of Human Resources so that the details of your appointment may be properly documented.

Congratulations Jessica! All of us here at MedWay Systems Inc. look forward to continuing to work with you in the future.

Sincerely,

Sharon Smithson
Manager, Customer Support Group

Actually, I was overly generous in the example I gave on the previous page. I provided much more information in the template than is normally included in a typical fill-in-the-blank template. They typically consist of two or three short generic statements with a bunch of blanks to fill in. Not much help in my opinion.

To see a direct comparison of real-life templates with fill-in-the-blank models go to:
http://instantbusinessletterkit.com/compare-templates.html

Advantages Of Real-Life Templates

Clearly, there can be no doubt that the "model" that most of us would rather work with if we had to write a similar letter is definitely the second one, the "real-life" template.

That's because you can relate to it. It talks about real-life people in a real-life situation that you can identify with. And, you get to see exactly how a professional writer worded it in a particular context.

Following, are the main advantages of "real-life" templates.

Content With Value

Working with "real-life" templates, it is much easier to adapt them to YOUR actual situations because they give you visual and intellectual cues to which you can relate.

Naturally, when you see how a copywriter or consultant has dealt with a "real-life" scenario, in terms of word choice, context, and punctuation, it is much easier to adapt effectively to the real-life situation for which you are writing. In that way, the actual content has value.

Easy To Work With

"Real-life" templates are just as easy to work with as the other templates. You simply load them into your word processing program and edit and adjust them to fit your own specific situation.

Presto! You have a fully formatted real-life letter ready to be printed and sent out in the mail.

You also have the comfort of knowing that what you are sending has already been used in other "real-life" situations, and it is grammatically correct.

Real-Life Content

With real-life templates, it is much easier to find an adaptable "fit" for the situation you are writing for. Not only do they give you the final format of a document, their content provides an excellent real-life sample and gives food-for-thought to assist you in the writing process.

Fully-Formatted Final Versions

"Real-life" templates are fully-formatted as final documents so that you can see exactly what they looked like when they were sent out in "real-life" situations. They don't look like some kind of "draft" computer-generated form letter.

Go ahead. Browse the sample letter templates found later in this guide. (see pg. 71).

Are you back yet? Ok.

Now I ask you, would you rather work from a "fill-in-the-blanks" generic template or from a fully-formatted "real-life" template?

I have no doubt that the vast majority of readers would choose the latter for all of the reasons given earlier. In fact, visitors to my Websites have already confirmed that.

Reality Check

All of the sample templates presented in this Kit are based on real-life situations using real-life content, for all of the reasons described above.

However, names, addresses, phone numbers, etc. that could be used to specifically identify an individual have been altered to protect privacy.

Working With Real-Life Templates

Let me take just a minute here to make sure you understand EXACTLY what you are getting with the "fully-formatted real-life templates" in this Kit. Here's the story...

If you purchased the e-book version of *Instant Business Letter Kit*, you also received a set of real-life word processing templates. (*If you bought the paperback version of the book, go to the Special Preface to find out how to get the templates by e-mail*).

With the templates you have a virtual "writing toolkit" packed with 127 fully-formatted real-life letters that you can download straight into your word processing program!

That's right; all of the templates included in this e-book have also being given to you in downloadable form in another file (MS-Word compatible).

Here's how you use those templates in a typical situation...

1. You have to write a business letter in a hurry.

2. You check the e-book and find the template that most closely fits your situation.

3. You open that specific template right into your word processing program!

4. You copy, cut, and paste a few revisions to transform the template **to fit your specific situation.**

PRESTO! You've got your fully-formatted, professional-quality final letter all ready-to-go in finished form, just like a real professional would write it.

Just think of the writing power this gives you!

No more laborious retyping/recopying from scratch. It's an instant document creator.

This is the power and the beauty of "real-life downloadable templates."

Using real-life templates, it shouldn't take you more than a few minutes to draft professional quality business letters that cover your specific situation.

The section of this manual titled "Use the Template Adaptation Method" (page 63) explains, in step-by-step detail, how you can quickly and easily adapt any real-life letter template in this Kit to draft a letter to fit your own specific situation.

WARNING: BEWARE OF AUTOMATIC LETTER GENERATORS

If you spend time online looking for letter writing help you will no doubt come across software programs that are claimed to "automatically generate" various types of letters.

All I can say about these products is "buyer beware"! Although it might have seemed like a good idea at the time, these "software letter generators" are only slightly better than the typical fill-in-the-bank templates.

Why, you ask? Here are the problems with the typical letter-writing software:

- For each letter type; you get to choose from about a half dozen or so "standard" pre-written one-liner phrases which you can plug into your letter.

- You do not get in-context mental stimulation and visual cues to help you visualize the finished product, the way that a real-life template does.

- The final software-generated-letter is a disjointed collection of weakly-linked sentences and paragraphs that actually needs a professional editing job just to make it presentable before sending it out.

To see a direct comparison of real-life templates with fill-in-the-blank models go to: http://instantbusinessletterkit.com/compare-templates.html

As I said, software letter generators might seem like a good idea, but they just don't do the job of a real-life template.

LETTER WRITING GUIDELINES - GENERAL

Even though this guide is written specifically to cover the writing of business letters, many of the basic principles of letter-writing in general apply and should be observed when writing all types of letters.

Based on the feedback that I get from visitors to the writinghelp-central.com site, letter writing is definitely the area where most people are looking for help or guidance.

In fact, over 60% of the visitors to my site are seeking some sort of letter writing information or assistance. And, as I stated earlier, a large number of them are looking for information related to writing business letters (second only to recommendation letters).

This section provides a brief review of the most important guidelines to follow when writing letters of any type. They are also generally applicable to writing business letters.

A later section of this guide includes guidelines and tips specific to the writing of business letters.

The following is a revised and expanded version of an article I wrote a few years ago, titled *"7 Essential Letter-Writing Strategies"*. That article was published in numerous eZines and posted on numerous websites across the Internet.

LETTER WRITING TIPS AND STRATEGIES

General Letter-Writing – Tips and Pointers

Following are a few practical letter writing tips adapted from the writinghelp-central.com Website to help you when writing that next letter:

Keep It Short and To The Point

Letters involving business (both personal and corporate) should be concise, factual, and focused. Try to never exceed one page or you will be at risk of losing your reader. A typical letter page will hold 350 to 400 words.

If you can't get your point across with that many words you probably haven't done enough preparatory work. If necessary, call the recipient on the phone to clarify any fuzzy points and then use the letter just to summarize the overall situation.

Focus On the Recipient's Needs

While writing the letter, focus on the information requirements of your audience, the intended addressee. If you can; in your "mind's eye" imagine the intended recipient seated across a desk or boardroom table from you while you are explaining the subject of the letter to them.

What essential information does that person need to know through this communication? What will be their expectations when they open the letter? Have these points all been addressed?

Use Simple and Appropriate Language

For clarity and precision, your letter should use simple straightforward language. Use short sentences and don't let paragraphs exceed three or four sentences. As much as possible, use language and terminology familiar to the intended recipient.

Don't use technical terms and acronyms without explaining them, unless you're certain the addressee is familiar with them.

Reread and Revise It

Do a first draft, and then carefully review and revise it. Put yourself in the place of the addressee. Imagine yourself receiving the letter. How would you react to it? Would it answer all of your questions? Does it deal with all of the key issues? Are the language and tone appropriate?

Sometimes reading it out loud to one's self can be a big help. When you actually "hear" the words, it is easy to tell if it "sounds" right, or not. I do this all the time and it really does work.

Eliminate Redundant Words and Phrases

There are certain words and phrases that one often sees in business correspondence that tend to make the language more complicated and cumbersome than necessary.

For example, some typical redundant words and phrases would include: "absolutely essential" instead of "essential", "actual experience" instead of "experience", "attached hereto" instead of "attached", "as a result of" instead of "because", "few in number" instead of "few", etc.

These are just a few examples. I'm sure you can think of others. Always look for redundant words/phrases when reviewing your final draft letter. **If a word or phrase doesn't add value and/or meaning, omit it.**

The chapter later on that deals with writing business letters specifically, contains a detailed write-up on "eliminating redundant words and phrases" (see page 55).

Use Transition Words and Phrases

One method that I always use to help with the flow and sequencing of my text in letters is to employ "transition words and phrases".

These are great for allowing you to connect thoughts and create logical sequences between sentences and paragraphs.

These words and phrases are usually inserted at the beginning of a sentence and they refer directly back to the previous sentence and/or paragraph without repeating the specific subject. They allow you to maintain a logical flow and make smooth transitions from one thought to the next.

Some typical transition words/phrases are: then, as a result, unlike, different, in spite of, next, in addition, like, the same, similar, for example, one such, for instance, accordingly, etc.

When using transition words/phrases, remember that they almost always *refer back* to the previous sentence or paragraph.

The chapter later on that deals with writing business letters specifically, contains a detailed write-up on the subject of "using transition words and phrases" (see page 58).

Check Spelling and Grammar

A letter is a direct reflection of the person sending it, and by extension, the organization that person works for. When the final content of the letter is settled, make sure that you run it through a spelling and grammar checker.

To send a letter with obvious spelling and grammatical errors is sloppy and unprofessional. In such cases, the recipient can't really be blamed for seeing this as an indication as to how you (and/or your organization) probably do most other things.

Spell-checkers are great, but they don't catch everything. For example, I often reverse the letters in certain words when typing quickly. i.e. "form" instead of "from." A typical spell-checker would say these are both valid words. Some grammar checkers will flag it as "out of context", but you can't always count on that.

The only way to be sure in the end that everything is fine, is to have someone with good spelling and grammar skills do a final check.

Bottom Line:

The foregoing general letter writing tips are mostly common sense. Nevertheless, **you would be amazed** at how often these very basic "rules of thumb" are not employed when people are writing letters.

BUSINESS LETTERS DEFINED

As I mentioned earlier, information about how to write business letters is the second most sought-after info at my writing help websites.

In the Introduction I pointed out the fact that there is a lot of confusion as to what exactly constitutes a true business letter. Indeed, if one checks out many "how to" reference guides on writing business letters, this confusion becomes apparent.

Often, these guides include just about every type of letter imaginable all mixed in together and very loosely labeled as "business" letters. They probably did this because the publisher told them that the term "business letters" would sell better than "general letters".

Unfortunately, such guides lack focus and are all over the place. On the other hand, this guide you are reading right now is "strictly business", so to speak.

This section contains a revised and expanded version of an article I penned a few years ago titled, *"Writing Business Letters That Get The Job Done"*. That article has been published in numerous e-Zines and is posted on numerous websites across the Internet.

BUSINESS LETTERS EXPLAINED

My two "writing help" websites receive well over two million visitors per year looking for information and templates to help them with their writing. With that many visitors I get a pretty accurate idea of exactly what people are looking for in the way of letter writing help. In fact, a significant number of people arrive at my site based on the search phrase "business letter".

Now, at first glance the term "business letter" makes sense. But, just wait a minute here! What exactly do they mean by "business letter"? Well, it turns out that they're not sure. What it boils down to in many cases is that the person doing the search is involved in some kind of "business" (as owner or employee) and they need to write some kind of "letter" related to their business. Hence, their search phrase of "business letter".

I often get e-mails from people asking me if I have any business letter templates, or if I can write them a business letter. Invariably, I have to reply to them asking "what type of business letter, what is the specific purpose"? The fact is; "business letter" is a very general term that can mean one of many different specific letter types.

Accordingly, the rest of this article is going to explain exactly what business letters are.

Despite the widespread use of e-mail in commerce today, traditional business letters are still the main way that the majority of businesses officially communicate with their customers and other businesses.

This is especially true when businesses want to formalize an agreement or an understanding. So far, emails are great for all of the preparatory work, but a formal business letter is still most often needed to "seal the deal".

There are two overall categories of business letters: business-to-business, and business-to-customer.

Business-To-Business Letters

Most business-to-business letters are written to confirm things that have already been discussed among officials in meetings, on the telephone, or via e-mail.

Can you imagine the letters that would have to go back and forth to cover all of the questions and possibilities that can be covered in a one-hour meeting, a half-hour phone call, or a few quick e-mails or texts?

The main purpose of a typical business letter is to formalize the details that were arrived at in those discussions, and to provide any additional information that was agreed upon.

Over the years, certain general standards have evolved in the business world that the vast majority of businesses use in drafting their business to business correspondence.

The Top 10 business-to-business letters that people search for at my writing help websites, in order of popularity, are as follows:

1. thank you letter
2. introduction letter
3. cover letter
4. financial letter
5. marketing letter
6. sales letter
7. project letter
8. invitation letter
9. employee letter
10. congratulations letter

Even though the above terms are much more specific than the general term "business letter" there are multiple types of each of the above letters, depending on the purpose of the letter. For example, a business-to-business "financial letter" could be: collection letter, credit approval letter, credit refusal letter, invoice, price quotation, etc.

Business-To-Customer Letters

There are many different types of business-to-customer letters. They include: sales and marketing letters, information letters, order acknowledgement letters, order status letters, collection letters, among others.

As with business-to-business letters, over the years certain general standards have evolved in the business world that the vast majority of businesses use in drafting letters to existing and potential customers.

Of course, going in the other direction are customer-to-business letters. These include: order letters, order status inquiry letters, complaint letters, and others.

Since these are customer-generated letters, there is no particular expectation that they follow any particular letter- writing standard. Typically, they are handled just like any other piece of personal correspondence.

The Top 10 business-to-customer letters that people search for at my writing help websites, in order of popularity, are as follows:

1. cover letter
2. customer relations letter
3. financial letter
4. credit letter
5. introduction letter
6. order-status letter
7. sales letter
8. marketing letter
9. announcement letter
10. apology letter

Even though the above business-to-customer letter types are much more specific than the general term "business letter", there are also multiple types of each of the above letters, depending on the purpose of the letter. For example, a business-to-customer "customer relations letter" could be any one of : response to a complaint, follow-up with a new customer, interrupted service notice, letter of acknowledgement, special invitation, welcome to new customers, etc.

Bottom-Line On Business Letters

As you can see from the above, specifying that you are looking for a "business letter" is not very enlightening. You need to be very specific and define the purpose of the letter; that is, exactly what is the letter meant to communicate?

It's important not to confuse non-business letters with business letters. That is; job application letters, resume cover letters, employment and college recommendation letters, character references, resignation letters, etc. are NOT truly business letters.

You might be surprised to learn that over 75% of all visitors to my main writing help website are searching for information on how to write just the Top 20 letters included in the lists above. In fact, it turns out that a full 90% of the more than 1 million people that visit that site each year searching for letter writing help are looking for help with one of a list of about 25 letters.

That's why all of my letter writing toolkits focus on multiple variations of about 40 specific letter types that cover over 97% of ALL letters ever written.

BUSINESS LETTER FORMATS

BASIC BUSINESS LETTER – LAYOUT

LETTERHEAD BLOCK
1234 Anyold Street., Suite 0000
Anyoldtown, XX, 00000
Tel. (000) 000-0000   Fax. (000) 000-0000

inbox@company.com   www.company.com

Date Line:

Address Block:
Address Block Line 2
Address Block Line 3
Address Block Line 4

Attention Line: *(optional)*

Salutation Line:

Subject Line: *(optional)*

Body Block: Paragraph 1. The primary purpose of a business letter is to convey a message that is worth writing down, clearly and succinctly, using as few words as possible, but without obscuring or diluting the main point(s).

Paragraph 2. The primary purpose of a business letter is to convey a message that is worth writing down, clearly and succinctly, using as few words as possible, but without obscuring or watering down the main point(s).

Paragraph 3. The primary purpose of a business letter is to convey a message that is worth writing down, clearly and succinctly, using as few words as possible, but without obscuring or watering down the main point(s).

Closing paragraph. This is usually a one or two sentence summary of the main point of the letter with a see you soon or thank you statement worked into it.

Complimentary Closing:

Signature Block: Name Line
Signature Block: Title Line

Reference Initials: *(optional)*

Enclosure/Attachment Line: *(when needed)*
cc Line: *(when needed)*

PARTS OF A BUSINESS LETTER

Depending on which letter writing textbook you refer to, the number and the names of the various formats will differ. Again, there seems to be no general international standard to use for writing business letters.

With direct reference to the terms marked in bold on the diagram on the previous page, here are definitions and explanations for the contents of each component part; starting at the top of the diagram and working to the bottom.

Letterhead Block:

All business letters should be composed and printed on Business Letterhead Paper. The letterhead block normally contains the company logo and all of its mailing and telephone co-ordinates. These days, the main e-mail address and the corporate website URL are also included in the letterhead block. Letterhead paper is often pre-printed, or the letterhead can be set-up as a template in a word processing program and printed out when each letter is printed.

Date Line:

The date that the letter is to be sent in full date form (e.g. October 28, 20XX). Make sure the date on the final version is the "official" sending date, and not one carried over from one of the earlier drafts.

Recipient Address Block:

This is the full mailing address of the recipient or addressee. This is the same address that will appear on the outside of the envelope.

Attention Line:

Optional. Used when a letter is addressed to a company in general but you want to make absolutely sure that it ends up on the desk of a specific individual. When used, this line is usually bolded and/or underlined for emphasis.

Salutation Line:

This is where you formally address the intended recipient. Make a point always to use a complete name here (i.e. first and last). If you don't have a specific name, telephone or e-mail the company and ask them to whom the letter should be addressed. Normally you should prefix the name with "Dear:" I normally use both names of the recipient in a business letter salutation, e.g. "Dear Mavis Strong:" If it just so happens that you know the recipient personally, you can handwrite on the letter as follows. With your pen, stroke out the person's name in the salutation line with a single horizontal stroke, and then hand-write their first name just above it to give it a personal touch. That way the letter still remains a piece of formal business correspondence, but you have added a personal touch to recognize your friendship with the recipient. There may be rare instances when you just can't get the complete recipient information; in which case you can use the standard anonymous salutation "To Whom It May Concern:"

Subject Line:

Optional. I use one whenever it makes sense because it cuts to the point and focus of the letter immediately. If worded properly it will save a lot of explanation in the body of the letter. In other words, a well-worded subject line can easily save one or two sentences in the body of the letter. This line is usually bolded and/or underlined for emphasis. It is sometimes typed in capital letters, although I don't think this is necessary with bolding and/or underlining.

Body Block:

This is the actual content of the letter. It should be single-spaced with an extra space between each paragraph. As stated elsewhere, the body should be three for four paragraphs of two or three sentences each.

As discussed in earlier sections of this guide, the objective when writing a business letter should always be to limit the letter to one page, if at all possible.

Complimentary Closing:

This should be polite and somewhat formal. The two most popular closing salutations for business letters are "Yours truly" and "Yours sincerely". Personally, I prefer one simple word to close most business letters - "Sincerely,". As far as I'm concerned, that says it all. In my opinion the "Yours" part is old fashioned, redundant and overly familiar. In fact, I only use the "Yours" part when it is someone who I know AND like (or if I *really* need their help or co-operation). Otherwise, I stick strictly with the arm's-length, "Sincerely".

Signature Block:

This is where the person writing the letter signs it by hand. It should include their full name on one line with their official business title on the next line, left-justified, right under the name. Three or four blank lines should be left between the complimentary closing and this block to give the sender room to sign their signature in longhand.

Reference Initials:

Optional: This is essentially the "audit trail" for the letter so that it's exact origins can be traced back, if ever needed. It is usually typed in the form "PF/sd" where "PF" are the initials of the person who drafted the letter, and "sd" are those of the person who typed it. Note that the drafter of the letter will not always be the person who signs it. Always insert the initials of the actual drafter. For example, if you draft a letter for your boss' signature, your own initials should be typed as the first pair of reference initials.

Enclosure/Attachment Line:

When needed: This is where you indicate whether the letter has enclosures and/or attachments. If there are enclosures included in the envelope with the letter, the term "Enclosure" should be used. It can be abbreviated as "Encl.". If there is something physically attached to the letter (i.e. stapled to it), that should be indicated here by using the term "Attachment". It can be abbreviated as "Attach:". Normally, if there are multiple Enclosures or Attachments, the number of such is usually specified in brackets. For example: Enclosures (3).

CC: Line:

When needed: CC stands for "carbon copy". This term is a carryover from the past. Although they aren't exactly "carbon" copies anymore, this simply refers to the formal distribution of any additional copies of the letter. This is normally used in situations where there are more than two parties directly involved in an issue, in addition to the sender and the recipient of the letter. For example, say you are chairperson of a four person committee and you have been directed to submit a progress report to your immediate boss. In such a case, you would be the sender, your boss the recipient, and the cc: copies would be shown on the cc: line as going to your fellow committee members.

NOTES:

Please note that a number of the business letter parts defined and described above are marked as "optional' or "when needed".

"Optional" means that it is your choice whether to use that particular feature, or not. Generally speaking, use an optional feature whenever you think it will improve the effectiveness of your message.

For example, a carefully worded Subject Line can create a specific focus and could reduce the length of your letter by one or two sentences

"When needed" means the same as "when applicable". Use these features whenever the situation calls for it.

That is, if you are sending copies of your letter to people other than the recipient you should always use the "CC: Line".

BUSINESS LETTER LAYOUT STYLES

Let me start this section by qualifying that this is not "the" all-encompassing definitive list of all possible business letter formats that are out there.

The books in my personal collection of style and business writing guides alone list at least a dozen different format variations for business letters. A number of them even refer to the same format using a variety of different names.

So, what I have done here is to simplify things as much as possible, and put together what I believe to be the most representative examples of business letter formats that are being used today, and then put my own stamp on them.

Here are what I consider to be the five generally accepted business letter formats or styles generally used in business today:

- Basic-Block
- Semi-Block
- Full-Block
- Square-Block
- Simplified Letter

The following is a very good online resource that goes into the technical details of most of these business letter styles and gives an idea of some of the differences in formats.
http://jobsearchtech.about.com/library/bl-business-letter-samples.htm

For the purposes of this guide, an illustration of the layout of each of the above-listed letter formats is provided on the following pages. In the first paragraph in the body text of each one, I briefly describe the characteristics of that particular layout so you can easily spot the differences.

After these format examples are presented, I will tell you which one is my preferred style – the one that I will stick with for the rest of this manual.

Basic-Block Style

CORPORATE LETTERHEAD INC.
4300 Davidson Blvd., Suite 1200

Princeton, NJ, 08550

Tel. (201) 345-1986   Fax. (201) 345-1998

info@corpletinc.com   www.corpletterhead.com

[Letter Date]

[Recipient Address]
[Address Line 2]
[Address Line 3]
[Address Line 4]

Attention: [*Optional Name*]

Dear [Recipient's Name]:

[Subject Line - *Optional:* **Usually Bold, Sometimes Underlined]**

The main attribute of the **Basic-Block style** is that everything is justified flush left except for the Date Line and Signature Block which are indented far right and aligned with each other on the left as shown. This style is somewhat outdated and has generally been replaced by the full-block or semi-block styles.

This is paragraph 2 of the actual content of the letter. As stated elsewhere, ideally this should be three for four paragraphs long, and kept short enough that the letter can fit onto one page.

This is paragraph 3 of the actual content of the letter. As stated elsewhere, ideally this should be three for four paragraphs long, and kept short enough that the letter can fit onto one page.

Closing paragraph. This is usually a one or two sentence summary of the main point of the letter with a "see you soon" or "thank you" statement included. See the templates later.

Sincerely,

[Name of Signatory]
[Title of Signatory]

[Reference Initials]

Enclosures: [number]

cc: [Name receiving copy]

[Name receiving copy]

Semi-Block Style

CORPORATE LETTERHEAD INC.
4300 Davidson Blvd., Suite 1200
Princeton, NJ, 08550
Tel. (201) 345-1986   Fax. (201) 345-1998

info@corpletinc.com   www.corpletterhead.com

[Letter Date]

[Recipient Address]
[Address Line 2]
[Address Line 3]
[Address Line 4]

Attention: [*Optional Name*]

Dear [Recipient's Name]:

[Subject Line - *Optional:* Usually Bold, Sometimes Underlined]

    The **Semi-Block style** is the same as the block-style except that the paragraphs are indented as shown. This style is somewhat outdated and has generally been replaced by the full-block or semi-block styles.

    This is paragraph 2 of the actual content of the letter. As stated elsewhere, ideally this should be three for four paragraphs long, and kept short enough that the letter can fit onto one page.

    This is paragraph 3 of the actual content of the letter. As stated elsewhere, ideally this should be three for four paragraphs long, and kept short enough that the letter can fit onto one page.

    Closing paragraph. This is usually a one or two sentence summary of the main point of the letter with a "see you soon" or "thank you" statement included. See the templates later.

Sincerely,

[Name of Signatory]
[Title of Signatory]

[Reference Initials]

Enclosures: [number]

cc: [Name receiving copy]
    [Name receiving copy]

Full-Block Style

CORPORATE LETTERHEAD INC.
4300 Davidson Blvd., Suite 1200

Princeton, NJ, 08550

Tel. (201) 345-1986   Fax. (201) 345-1998

info@corpletinc.com   www.corpletterhead.com

[Letter Date]

[Recipient Address]
[Address Line 2]
[Address Line 3]
[Address Line 4]

Attention: [*Optional Name*]

Dear [Recipient's Name]:

[Subject Line - *Optional:* Usually Bold, Sometimes Underlined]

The main attribute of the **Full-Block style** is that everything is justified flush left. This is considered to be the most formal style. Even so, it is my personal favorite since I think it has a clean, uncluttered, and efficient, business-like look.

This is paragraph 2 of the actual content of the letter. As stated elsewhere, ideally this should be three for four paragraphs long, and kept short enough that the letter can fit onto one page.

This is paragraph 3 of the actual content of the letter. As stated elsewhere, ideally this should be three for four paragraphs long, and kept short enough that the letter can fit onto one page.

Closing paragraph. This is usually a one or two sentence summary of the main point of the letter with a "see you soon" or "thank you" statement included. See the templates later.

Sincerely,

[Name of Signatory]
[Title of Signatory]

[Reference Initials]

Enclosures: [number]

cc: [Name receiving copy]
    [Name receiving copy]

Square-Block Style

CORPORATE LETTERHEAD INC.

4300 Davidson Blvd., Suite 1200

Princeton, NJ, 08550

Tel. (201) 345-1986   Fax. (201) 345-1998

info@corpletinc.com   www.corpletterhead.com

[Recipient Address]   [Letter Date]
[Address Line 2]
[Address Line 3]
[Address Line 4]

Attention: *[Optional - Name]*

Dear [Recipient's Name]:

[Subject Line - *Optional:* Usually Bold And Is Sometimes Underlined]

The **Square-Block style** is called that because it actually has a "squarish" appearance due to the left and right justification of certain lines of text. Recipient Address and Signature Block are left-justified, while Date and Reference Initials are right-justified.

This is paragraph 2 of the actual content of the letter. As stated elsewhere, ideally this should be three or four paragraphs long, and kept short enough that the letter can fit onto one page.

This is paragraph 3 of the actual content of the letter. As stated elsewhere, ideally this should be three for four paragraphs long, and kept short enough that the letter can fit onto one page.

Closing paragraph. This is usually a one or two sentence summary of the main point of the letter with a "see you soon" or "thank you" statement included. See the templates later.

Sincerely,

[Name of Signatory]   [Reference Initials]
[Title of Signatory]

Enclosures: [number]

cc: [Name receiving copy]

   [Name receiving copy]

Simplified Letter Style

<hr>

CORPORATE LETTERHEAD INC.
4300 Davidson Blvd., Suite 1200
Princeton, NJ, 08550
Tel. (201) 345-1986 Fax. (201) 345-1998

info@corpletinc.com   www.corpletterhead.com

[Letter Date]

[Recipient Address]
[Address Line 2]
[Address Line 3]
[Address Line 4]

[Subject Line - *Optional:* **Usually Bold And Is Sometimes Underlined]**

The **Simplified Letter style** is used in straightforward situations such as simple announcements of events. They do not normally include the usual opening and closing salutation blocks. The subject line is often centered.

This is paragraph 2 of the actual content of the letter. As stated elsewhere, ideally this should be three for four paragraphs long, and kept short enough that the letter can fit onto one page.

This is paragraph 3 of the actual content of the letter. As stated elsewhere, ideally this should be three for four paragraphs long, and kept short enough that the letter can fit onto one page.

Closing paragraph. This is usually a one or two sentence summary of the main point of the letter with a see you soon or thank you statement worked into it. See the templates later.

[Name of Signatory], [Title of Signatory]

[Reference Initials]

Enclosures: [number]

<hr>

Continuation Page

Page [nn]
[Recipient Name]
[Letter Date]

The only thing that is different on the **continuation page** is the inclusion of the Page Number, Recipient Name, and Date, four or five spaces down from the top left-hand margin of the letter page. The remainder of the page should be formatted just like the first page, and the letter will conclude just as if it was finishing on the first page.

Business Envelope Format

The address on the envelope should match the recipient address in the Address Block of the letter. The address and return address should be positioned as shown in the diagram below. The main address block should start 4 inches from the left-edge of the envelope and about 1.5 inches from the top edge. In most jurisdictions, the postal or ZIP code should be the last item printed so that sorting machines can process the letter properly.

Most businesses have envelopes pre-printed with their logo and return address co-ordinates appearing in the upper left-hand corner.

Return Address Block
Return Address Line 2
Return Address Line 3
Return Address Line 4

                    Recipient Address Block
                    Recipient Address Line 2
                    Recipient Address Line 3
                    Recipient Address Line 4
                    Postal Code Line

The standard business envelope used in North America is a #10 white vellum envelope, measuring 4 1/8 in. by 9 ½ in.

BUSINESS LETTER FORMATTING GUIDELINES

General Formatting Guidelines

These are recommended formatting guidelines only. Nothing here is cast in concrete.

Vary them as you see fit, within reason; or as you may require in order to "squeeze" things onto one page. Remember, if you do "squeeze" things a bit, it shouldn't be easily detectable by the average reader.

In other words, it shouldn't "look" squeezed. If it does, you will have to go to a second page (See the following section for tips on "compressing" a letter onto one page).

- Top and bottom, and left and right page margins, can vary from 1 in. to 1.5 in. but should be (or, appear to be) the same all the way around.

- I recommend using a font style and size of Times Roman, 12 point. This combination has a businesslike appearance and is widely used.

- The main text of business letters should be single spaced, with double spacing between paragraphs.

- A typical one-page business letter will have between four (4) and (5) paragraphs. Try to limit paragraphs to two or three sentences each in order to achieve a balanced look that is not too dense.

- Generally speaking, skip one (1) line horizontally between the different components of the letter (as per sample formats).

- At the top of the letter, try to skip between two (2) and three (3) lines between the Letterhead Block and the Recipient Address Block.

- In the Signature Block, leave three (3) to four (4) lines between the Closing Salutation (i.e. Sincerely), and the Signatory Name so that there is ample room for a normal hand-written signature.

- For a general idea of spacing, refer to the sample formats presented earlier in this chapter. The most important thing is "relative" spacing. It is not hard to recognize when two items are too close together or too far apart.

- After you have finished the letter you may want to make some final adjustments to spacing in order to give it a "balanced" look.

In my experience, the spacing in business letters is not an "exact science" (if it ever was). What you're looking for is an uncluttered, balanced look that respects the basic format you are following (as per the earlier samples).

So, don't get too worked-up about absolute formatting perfection!

I've written more business letters than I care to remember over the years and I can't recall one of them ever being ignored because the margins were 0.8" rather than 1.0".

If it's uncluttered and well-balanced in appearance (and most importantly, well-written!), it will be taken seriously as a professional business letter.

As far as punctuation and capitalization are concerned, please refer to the "real-life templates" used throughout this guide to see specific examples in specific contexts.

You can also check with any one of the writing guides listed under "Business Writing References" in the Resources chapter at the end of this guide. (see pg. 261).

Tricks For Keeping A Letter On One Page

There are a number of handy little tricks that I have developed over the years that will help you compress or "squeeze" a letter onto one page without it being noticed by the average reader. These tricks can be applied using any standard word processing software program.

I'm not sure whether a purist at a secretarial school would approve of some of my methods since they may deviate somewhat from certain standards, but I have used them hundreds of times and nobody has ever been the wiser. The main point is that I was able to keep a letter on one page when the first version overflowed by a few lines onto a second page.

Below are my "page compression tips", in the order I suggest you use them:

1. Move both the left and right margins out about ¼ in. closer to the edge of the page.

2. Move the top and bottom margins out about ¼ in. closer to the edge of the page.

3. Edit out the one or two word "overflows". What I mean here is this. After the letter is drafted take a good look at each paragraph. See if there are any that have an ending sentence that "overflows" into an additional line for the sake of one word. If so, make a minor edit or two in the paragraph that shortens it a little so that that last word or two will not overflow onto the following line. Using this method, you can often gain two or three extra lines in a one-page letter.

4. Adjust the line-spacing on the page. You can gain considerable space on a page by adjusting the line spacing of the text. For example, if the default line spacing is set to "single" at 12 points try setting it to "exactly" at 12 points if your font size is 12. If that doesn't do it, try "exactly" at "11 pts". Often you have to experiment a bit with this one to get the look just right.

5. As a last resort, try reducing the font size by 1 point, say from 12 to 11 pts.

6. If it still doesn't "fit", there's one final thing you can try if you're the author of the letter. Go back and edit it one more time. Look for redundant thoughts and phrases, or those that can be combined into one sentence rather than two. Is every word and phrase absolutely essential to your message? You'll be amazed at the space savings that this process can result in.

As I said earlier, try the above methods in sequence, one-at-a-time, checking each time to see if your latest change has done the trick for you.

So, what happens if it still won't fit?

Now, if you've used all of the above tricks and you still can't get the letter to fit onto one page, it's time to admit that you've got a real two-pager. In which case, you should then think about "reversing" some of the compression tricks that you applied when you tried to squeeze the letter. Then, focus on making a balanced looking second page.

There's nothing worse looking (or more unprofessional) than a letter with a one or two sentence second page! I'm sure you've seen them. So, if this is this case, even after trying the squeeze tricks above, you may want to actually "stretch" the letter out a bit.

Often, at this stage I actually increase the line-spacing and reduce the margins slightly so that there will be a decent sized overflow onto the second page.

For example, try reversing steps 1, 2 and 4 above. That is, instead of increasing the top, bottom and side margins on page one, try decreasing them by ¼ in. all around. Then adjust the point size and see if that helps.

Again, I have used these little "compression" tricks thousands of times, and nobody has ever pulled out their ruler and chastised me for inaccuracy.

In fact, if you did a detailed check on the business letter templates included throughout this guide you would find that I have used one or more of the above tricks on a number of them.

But, I'm not telling which ones!

THE BUSINESS MEMORANDUM

Purpose Of A Memo

The business memorandum is essentially an "internal" business letter.

The "memo" as it is usually called, is the key internal communication mechanism in most businesses. In fact, the business memo is arguably the most important communications instrument in an organization.

Memoranda are used to announce, inform, advise, quantify, delegate, direct, instruct, request, and transmit. In short, if something needs to be communicated and/or recorded formally "within" an organization, it is done with a memo.

Business memoranda make up an organization's official corporate record of business decisions made, actions taken, and policies implemented. In effect, the body of corporate memoranda for an organization is its corporate memory.

In many large organizations the corporate memorandum is the key "power instrument" when it comes to internal politics. Entire careers and multi-million dollar programs often hinge on the wording of a memo.

Memo Writing Guidelines

A memorandum is considered a formal business communication in the same way as a business letter. Even though it is an internal document, because it will become part of the corporate record of an organization it needs to be well written.

The guidelines given in the previous sections of this guide for the writing of business letters would also apply to writing business memoranda. Most large organizations have their own corporate format for their memos. The following page contains a sample of a typical internal business memorandum.

When reviewing the sample memo, please note that I have included a Signature Line at the bottom. Many organizations do not require a Signature Line on a memo. On the other hand, I believe that a memo should have a signature on the bottom if it is to have maximum impact and credibility.

Basic Memo Format

CORPORATE MEMORANDUM LETTERHEAD

MEMORANDUM

FILE NO: xxxxx-xxx

DATE: April 12, 20xx

TO: Name/Addressee 1, Name/Addressee 2, Name/Addressee 3,
Name/Addressee 4, Name/Addressee 5, Name/Addressee 6,
Name/Addressee 7, Name/Addressee 8

FROM: Stephen Jackson

SUBJECT: **Agenda For Strategic Planning Session – Tuesday April 18, 20xx**

Below is the final draft agenda for next week's all day strategic planning session:

Discussion Item	Time	Lead
1. Opening Remarks, Review Agenda	08:30 - 09:00	S. Jackson
2. Review/Refine Mission Statement	09:00 – 09:30	S. Jackson
3. Review/Revise Core Values	09:30 – 10:15	B. Kumar
Refreshment Break	1015 – 10:30	
4. Review/Revise Success Factors	10:30 – 11:15	B. Kumar
5. Identify/Define/Prioritize Strategic Issues	11:15 – 12:00	R. Tucker
Lunch Break	12:00 – 13:00	
6. Develop Strategic Objective Statements	13:00 – 14:00	R. Tucker
7. Identify Performance Indicators	14:00 – 15:00	B. Kumar
Refreshment Break	15:00 – 15:15	
8. Identify Action Plan Items	15:15 – 16:00	F. Campbell
9. Summary and Wrap-Up	16:00 – 16:30	S. Jackson

Could you please make sure that you review the discussion papers that were provided to you at last week's Management Meeting prior to the session. Also, please ensure you bring your copy of the current Strategic Plan to the session.

S. Jackson *(optional)*

c.c. R. Braithwaite

LETTER FORMAT USED IN THIS GUIDE

By definition, all of the sample letters and templates included in this Kit are business letters of one description or another. As already discussed, there are many possible formats or page layouts for business letters.

Depending on which letter writing text you reference, the number and names of the various formats will differ. There seems to be no general international standard for use when writing business letters.

Consequently, I have decided to use my personal favorite letter format in all of the templates/samples included throughout this document – *Full-Block Style*. As shown earlier, this style positions all major sections of the letter flush to the left-hand margin for a clean businesslike look (see sample layout, page 41).

CORPORATE CORRESPONDENCE MANUALS

Most large organizations and some smaller ones have a "corporate style manual" that specifies the standards for letters that are to be used in that organization.

At one point in my career I was asked to supervise the development of an "Executive Correspondence Manual" for a government agency. When completed, that document specified every detail imaginable for the writing and distribution of both internal and external correspondence generated in the Executive Branch of that agency. Eventually, it was adopted as the correspondence standard for the entire organization.

That manual specified such details as: paper size, color, thickness, and brightness, letter layouts, memo layouts, font styles, font sizes, line spacing, correspondence distribution and routing, filing procedures, acceptable and unacceptable corporate terminology, etc.

If your organization doesn't have such a manual, check around and you might be surprised to find a long-forgotten correspondence manual collecting dust somewhere. If you find one, you can use it as is, or recommend that it be revised if it is out of date.

Bottom line: If you are in a situation where there is no particular letter writing standard in-place in your organization, choose one style that you like and stick with it.

HOW TO WRITE BUSINESS LETTERS

In addition to general letter-writing protocols covered earlier (see page 25), there are a number of basic guidelines that cover most situations related to the writing of business letters specifically. These are usually more "situational" than "how to" in nature.

The following is an excerpt from an article I wrote a few years ago, titled *"Business Letter Writing Tips and Strategies."* That article was published in numerous e-Zines and can be found posted on various websites across the Internet.

BUSINESS LETTER WRITING TIPS AND STRATEGIES

The following tips apply primarily to the writing of business letters and memos as defined previously.

Business Letters - Tips and Tricks

Here are a few tips I have picked up while writing literally hundreds of business letters over the past 25+ years. This is a revised and updated version of the business writing tips included in my e-book, "Instant Home Writing Kit".

Limit Them to One Page
By definition, business letters should be short and to the point, preferably one page in length. Studies have found that busy business people do not like to read beyond the first page, and will actually delay reading longer letters. So, if you don't want your letter to gather dust in an in-basket, keep it as short as possible.

Be Reader Friendly
Always try to focus on the needs of the reader and make an effort to see things from their perspective. Put yourself in their position and imagine what it would be like receiving your letter. Everyone can do this, since we are all "customers" of some other business in some part of our lives.

Keep the Tone Formal and Factual

Generally speaking, the tone and content of business letters should be formal and factual. Feelings and emotions do not have a place in business letters. But don't overdo it. A cordial, friendly approach is fine. Just keep it businesslike, but avoid overly formal terms like "heretofor", "as per", "herewith", etc.

Carefully Plan Your Letter

Before writing the letter take a few minutes to list all of the specific points you need to cover. Sometimes it may even mean a call to the recipient or his/her company to confirm a specific point. Remember, the purpose of the letter is to tie up all of the details on the subject at hand, so that more letters won't have to be written back and forth.

Make It Clear, Concise and Logical

Use a clear and direct writing style that uses simple words and straightforward phrases. Make sure that your flow follows a logical progression, first identifying the main subject, elaborating on it, and then drawing the logical conclusion.

Accuracy and Timeliness are Important

By their very nature, business letters need to be accurate and timely. They almost always have financial implications and related impacts on other businesses and/or people. Double-check all of the facts stated in the letter, and make sure that any future dates specified give others enough time to realistically complete what is expected of them.

Relegate Technical Details to Attachments

Often, it is necessary to include detailed technical information as part of a business letter package. In such cases, use the main letter as a cover letter that lists and briefly explains and references the attached (or enclosed) documents.

Use Non-Discriminatory Language

Make sure that you avoid language that is specific to gender, race, or religion in all business letters, either to other businesses, or to customers. For example, use "workforce" instead of "manpower", or "chairperson" rather than "chairman". Most style guides contain detailed lists of the offensive terms and some suggested substitutes.

Eliminate Redundant Words and Phrases

There are certain words and phrases that one often sees in business correspondence that tend to make the language more complicated and cumbersome than necessary. The following table contains some of these with alternative wording provided.

Instead of this…	Use this…
absolutely essential	essential
accounted for	caused by
actual experience	experience
add the point that	add that
advise, inform	say, tell, let us know
along those lines	like, similar to
am in receipt of	have
are of the opinion of	think that, believe that
as a result of	because
as of this date	today
at your earliest convenience	soon, next week, specific date
at this time, at the present time	now, at present
attached hereto	attached
attached please find	attached is
came to the conclusion	concluded
check into	check
cancel out	cancel
cognizant	aware
collect together	collect
compensate	pay
conceive	think
consensus of opinion	consensus
conception	idea
conclude, conclusion	end
consequent results	results
connect up	connect
deficiency	lack
demonstrate	show
descend down	descend

Instead of this...	Use this...
despite the fact that	although
determine	find
discontinue	stop
due to the fact that	due to, because
early beginnings	beginnings
effect a change	change
enclosed herein	enclosed
encounter	meet
endeavor	try
equitable	fair
establish	set up
exemplify	show
exhibits a tendency to	tends to
facilitate	help
few in number	few
first and foremost	first
for the purpose of	for
for the reason that	because
forward	send
free of charge	free
frequently	often
give an indication of	indicate
have at hand	have
I am of the opinion	I think
in accordance with	according to
in advance of	before
inasmuch as	because
in compliance with	as requested, as specified
in spite of the fact that	although
in the amount of	for
in the course of	during
in the event that	if, in case
in the majority of cases	most, usually
in the matter of	about

Instead of this...	Use this...
in the process of being	being
in the near future	soon
in the neighborhood of	about
in the normal course of events	normally
in the same way as described	as described
in this day and age	nowadays
in view of the fact that	because
indicate	show
initiate	begin, start
is/was found to be	is/was
is suggestive of	suggests
it has been brought to my attention	I have learned
it is apparent that	it seems
join together	join
kindly	please
make a decision to	decide
make the acquaintance of	meet
mutual cooperation	cooperation
my personal opinion	my opinion
new innovation	new
of a confidential nature	confidential
on behalf of	for
on the basis of	by
on the grounds that	since
on the part of	by
owing to the fact that	because, since
past experience	experience
permit me to take this opportunity	I want to
pertaining to	about
perform an analysis of	analyze
perform an examination of	examine
preparatory to	before
present a conclusion	conclude
prior to	before

Instead of this...	Use this...
prolong the duration of	prolong
provided that	if
reached an agreement	agreed
send an answer	reply
the modifications contained herein	these changes
subsequent to	after, since
subsequently	later
supplement	add
take under advisement	consider
the undersigned	I, me
terminate	end, stop
the committee made the decision	the committee decided
the question as to whether	whether
to be in agreement with	agree
to have a preference for	prefer
to secure	to get
under no circumstances	never
undertake a study of	study
until such time as	until
utilize, utilization	use
with a view to	to
with regard to	about
within the realm of possibility	possible
whereas	but
whereby	which
whether or not	whether
you will find attached	attached is, here is

The above list is not exhaustive; it's the best that I could come up with when I wrote this chapter. But I'm sure you get the point. No doubt there are many more of these, and I urge you to be on the lookout for them.

The obvious lessons that one can draw from the above is: the simpler the better, and don't use three words when one or two will do the job.

Use Transition Words and Phrases

On a regular basis, I see business letters and reports in which each phrase seems to be independent of the one before and the one after, when in reality there is an actual sequential and/or logical flow.

Consider the following three sentence example:

1. The entire building had to be searched.
2. They started the search on the third floor.
3. It took three hours to complete the search.

Notice that the three separate statements are all valid sentences. They convey the bare essential facts of the situation, but nothing more. In fact, they raise almost more questions than they answer. For example:

- Was it a serious incident?
- Had it ever happened before?
- Why did they start on the third floor?
- What about the first two floors?
- How big/high was the building?
- Is three hours a long time for that?
- How long does it usually take?

These are all logical (and obvious) questions that the average person might easily wonder about when reading a paragraph made up of the three sentences above.

Let's transform these now, using some transition words/phrases:

> "UNLIKE the previous minor incident, this time the entire building had to be searched. BECAUSE the fire was still smoking on the first two floors, they had to start on the third, working upwards to the tenth, covering the first two floors last. CONSEQUENTLY, it took them a full three hours before they finally completed the typical two-hour job."

Notice the use of the transition words: UNLIKE, BECAUSE, and CONSEQUENTLY. Using these three words has allowed us to easily connect the three independent sentences and give them a sense of chronological order and logical flow. They also allow us to answer ALL of the obvious questions, either with the transition word itself, or by adding a couple more words.

In short, transition words/phrases have turned three dry independent phrases into a little story that makes sense to the reader.

These types of words/phrases are ideal for allowing one to easily connect thoughts, and create logical sequences between sentences and paragraphs. They are usually inserted at the beginning of a sentence and normally refer directly back to the previous sentence and/or paragraph without repeating the specific subject.

The following table lists some of the more common transition words and phrases that will help make your text more understandable and interesting to the reader. For each one, I have included a typical example of how the word/phrase might be used in a typical sentence.

Transition word or phrase…	**Sample sentence using the transition word/phrase…**
Cause and Effect	
then	*Then*, he moved to the next work station.
as a result	*As a result*, the team lost the game.
for this reason	*For this reason*, she always went home for the weekend.
the result was	*The result was* always predictable.
what followed	*What followed* was as painful as it was inevitable.
in response	*In response*, he upped the ante.
therefore	*Therefore*, the aircraft overshot the runway.
thus	*Thus*, it was just a matter of time.
because of	*Because of this*, the results were always the same.
consequently	*Consequently*, he was no longer friends with Frank.
the reaction	*The reaction* to this event was swift and decisive.

Transition word or phrase…	Sample sentence using the transition word/phrase…
In Contrast To unlike different in spite of on the other hand on the contrary opposing however contrary to nevertheless	*Unlike* last year, this one was highly profitable. *Different* from this, was our approach to manufacturing. *In spite of* the dot com bust, the company prospered. *On the other hand*, earnings per share have increased. *On the contrary*, the impact was less than expected. *Opposing* that idea was the move to new technologies. *However*, that approach may actually prove better. *Contrary to* his findings, the revenue picture is good. *Nevertheless*, something still appears to be missing.
Sequence and relativity then in addition to enumerate next next in the series besides that subsequently following	*Then*, each one followed in numerical order sequence. *In addition*, a fourth material was added to the mix. *To enumerate*, first there was the accident, then … *Next* in line for cuts was the marketing division. *Next in the series* was the "outrigger" brand line. *Besides* that, there were two other possible sources. *Subsequently*, they moved to the next step in the series. *Following* the concert, there was a reception in the lounge.
Similarity and Comparison like the same similar close likewise also near	Just *like* that, he took the company on a similar course. The new approach was almost exactly *the same*. *Similar* things were known to happen at certain times. The latest results were *close*, but far from perfect. *Likewise*, they made similar changes in the factory. *Also*, there were the worker's families to consider. *Near* that one, was the faulty component.

Transition word or phrase...	Sample sentence using the transition word/phrase...
Explanation and Example	
for example	*For example*, last year's model was underpowered.
one such	*One such* occurrence was last week's power outage.
for instance	*For instance*, earnings this year are higher than last.
to illustrate	*To illustrate*, he went to Chicago just to make his point.
also	*Also*, there is a new approach to sheet-metal moulding.
that too	*That too*, just goes to make my point even stronger.
to demonstrate	*To demonstrate*, I will use the new model throughout.

As shown in the examples, these words and phrases are usually inserted at the beginning of a sentence. They normally refer directly back to the previous sentence and/or paragraph without repeating the specific subject.

The above are just examples. There are many other such transition words and phrases used in everyday conversation and writing. I believe that appropriate use of such words and phrases is the number one technique for making any type of writing flow more logically and clearly.

Bottom line:

Smooth, orderly and logical transitions from one thought to another, one sentence to the next, and one paragraph to the other, are the key to creating clear flow and meaning in any document. Appropriate use of transition words and phrases will achieve this for you in your business letters.

USE THE "TEMPLATE ADAPTATION METHOD"

The Template Adaptation Method™ is an approach I developed years ago that allows you to easily use pre-written templates as a tool for developing your own letters, in no time flat.

Using this method in conjunction with real-life templates you will never have to start from a blank page or screen again. Not only will it significantly reduce the time taken to write your letter, it will also result in a better quality final product.

I'm about to give up a major "trade secret" here.

I first discovered the Template Adaptation Method™ years ago when I was in a job where I had to write a lot of letters and reports. At times, I suffered serious bouts of "writer's block". Sometimes I would stare at a blank page, screen and/or off into space for days. Yes, literally for days, sometimes.

Then one fateful day I had the proverbial "eureka experience" that changed my writing life forever! Really. I'm not sure whether it was by chance, or fluke, or divine intervention, but that particular day I stumbled onto a powerful secret for overcoming "writer's block" -- instantly.

As is usually the case when one makes one of these little "breakthroughs" in life, it was incredibly simple. It was so obvious.

So, here is the big secret that I discovered for beating writer's block:

Place an actual sample of the type of document you have to write, directly in your line-of-sight. The closer the sample is to what you have to write, the better. For example, if you have to write a reference letter, try to find a previous letter of reference that you have written. If you haven't done one before, get one that somebody else has written and post that up.

That's it! It really is that simple. I call it the "template adaptation method".

Don't ask me exactly how/why it works, but it does. My theory is that it gives your brain a concrete visual cue as to what you need to write in a very specific way. Staring at a blank page/monitor, or out into white space, just doesn't give you this kind of cue.

In fact, the very first thing I did when I sat in front of my computer to write this book was to open a copy of one of my previous books right into my word processor. I then placed a hard copy of that eBook on the book stand/easel to my left, right beside the computer monitor.

I was able to immediately start writing the new book on the spot using that "real-life template document" in my word processing program, and by referring to the hard copy document beside me, as required.

Although the final versions of the document have completely different content, that doesn't seem to matter, **because the structure and the flow are similar, and that seems to be the key.**

Using my Template Adaptation Method^{TM} for this book was a great time-saver. I'm sure it took about half the time it would have, working from a blank page/screen.

Not only that; it also allowed me to get started almost instantly.

So, if you are blocked at all in writing your own letters, and staring into space, or at a blank page or screen, I urge you to find an appropriate real-life template and give my "template adaptation method" a try. I guarantee, you'll be pleasantly surprised.

As I stated above, I personally use the Template Adaptation Method^{TM} all the time when I'm writing letters, essays, reports, and just about any other document.

In fact, thanks to this method, it is rare that I ever have to write anything anymore from a blank page or screen. And that's a great relief, I can tell you!

Before going further you might want to do a quick review of the earlier chapter that explains what "real-life temples" are all about. To most effectively utilize the template adaptation method, it is best to be working from a real-life template (see page 17).

A STEP-BY-STEP APPROACH

Here's a step-by-step way to apply the Template Adaptation Method™ in developing your own letters.

1. **First, scan through all of the sample letters** included in this guide and find one that is <u>closest</u> to what you need. Look at all the samples just to be sure. For example, if you need to write a recommendation letter you will want to check the reference letter samples as well to see if there's a better "fit" there.

2. **Once you've found a suitable letter template** "along the lines" of what you're looking for in approach and style; copy and paste it into your word processor.

3. **Start drafting your letter on the same page** as the one you just selected and pasted, one paragraph at a time. This point is very important. MAKE SURE you do it one paragraph at a time.

4. **Proceed through the entire document**, writing your letter, line-by-line, paragraph-by-paragraph, until you have progressed through the entire letter.

5. **Read through the paragraphs you have created** and make sure they make sense and flow smoothly and logically, roughly in step with the flow of the template.

6. **Now, delete all of the template paragraphs.** What will remain is your own personalized letter, but using the approach and style of the template.

On the following pages I give you an actual example that shows exactly how this Template Adaptation Method™ works, in practical terms.

A REAL-LIFE EXAMPLE

I'm going to give you a detailed example here so you will understand exactly what I'm talking about.

To keep things simple, I'll use the introduction letter template that is included later on in the chapter on Business-to-Business - Introduction Letters (see page 107). I chose that one because it represents a straightforward business letter-writing situation.

Here's the ORIGINAL real-life introduction letter template:

Dear Mr. Collinson:

The purpose of this letter is to briefly introduce myself as Dynatek's new Sales Representative, Business Accounts. I very recently joined the company and am taking over your account from Jack Winters who has moved on to other challenges in this industry.

I have just completed Dynatek's management orientation program and am now keen to meet face-to-face with all of my key customers.

Accordingly, as a first step in my customer familiarization process, I would like to meet with you personally, for about an hour or so, to discuss Office-Tech's needs and concerns. At the same time I would also like to take that opportunity to briefly review Dynatek's latest offering of products and services.

To set up a meeting for this at your convenience, I propose to call your office by the end of this week. It is my hope that we will be able to arrange to meet at your offices before the end of the month.

As your new Dynatek Business Account Representative I believe that my paramount concern is how both Dynatek Inc. and I can better serve Office-Tech Furnishings Inc.

I look forward to meeting with you and learning more about your company in the near future.

Sincerely,

Jim O'Malley
Senior Sales Representative

The above example is a typical business introduction letter written by someone who is new to a company and has taken over the accounts of his predecessor.

Now, here's the new introduction letter scenario for which you need a new letter:

- You have just replaced Lacey Williams at Godfrey Papers Inc. and you are in the process of contacting all of her clients whom you will now service.

- You want to get your letter out to all clients before the annual trade show which takes place in three weeks.

- You will be located at the Godfrey Papers booth (No. 417) and hope to meet as many of your new clients as possible so you can set up a follow-up meeting.

Now let's use the above template to create a new letter, paragraph by paragraph.

Paragraph 1 – Template Version:

Dear Mr. Collinson:

The purpose of this letter is to briefly introduce myself as Dynatek's new Sales Representative, Business Accounts. I very recently joined the company and am taking over your account from Jack Winters who has moved on to other challenges in this industry.

Paragraph 1 – New Version:

Dear Mr. Ortega:

My name is Frank Samson and I have recently become the Senior Client Representative for Godfrey Papers Inc. I have replaced Lacey Williams who I understand serviced your account for the past five years.

Paragraph 2 – Template Version:

I have just completed Dynatek's management orientation program and am now keen to meet face-to-face with all of my key customers.

Paragraph 2 – New Version:

Before joining Godfrey Papers, I worked for ten years as a key accounts manager for Quality Papers Consolidated, so I have a strong background in the fine papers industry.

Paragraph 3 – Template Version:

Accordingly, as a first step in my customer familiarization process, I would like to meet with you personally, for about an hour or so, to discuss Office-Tech's needs and concerns. At the same time I would also like to take that opportunity to briefly review Dynatek's latest offering of products and services.

Paragraph 3 – New Version:

Even though I am still in the process of familiarizing myself with your company's operations, I am contacting you at this point in the hope that we might be able to make our first contact at next month's Fine Papers International Trade Show -20xx. I intend to be stationed at Godfrey's kiosk throughout the show, where I hope to meet as many of my new client contacts as possible in person.

Paragraph 4 – Template Version:

To set up a meeting for this at your convenience, I propose to call your office by the end of this week. It is my hope that we will be able to arrange to meet at your offices before the end of the month.

Paragraph 4 – New Version:

If you do attend the show I would really appreciate it if you would be kind enough to drop by Booth 417 and introduce yourself. Perhaps at that time we can take the opportunity to set up an introductory marketing familiarization meeting for the near future. Also, while you are there you will be able to enter our draw for a giant plazma wide-screen TV.

Paragraph 5 – Template Version:

As your new Dynatek Business Account Representative I believe that my paramount concern is how both Dynatek Inc. and I can better serve Office-Tech Furnishings Inc.

Paragraph 5 – New Version:

As your new Godfrey Papers Inc. Client Representative I very much look forward to familiarizing myself with your company's operations so that I may serve you well.

Closing – Template Version:

I look forward to meeting with you and learning more about your company in the near future.

Closing – New Version:

I really hope that we will have an opportunity to get acquainted at the FPI show.

Now let's copy and paste all of the "New Version" paragraphs developed above into a new template and see what it looks like:

Here's the NEW ADAPTED version of the introduction letter:

Dear Mr Ortega:

My name is Frank Samson and I have recently become the Senior Client Representative for Godfrey Papers Inc. I have replaced Lacey Williams who I understand serviced your account for the past five years.

Before joining Godfrey, I worked for ten years as a key accounts manager for Quality Papers Consolidated so I have a strong background in the fine papers industry.

Even though I am still in the process of familiarizing myself with your company's operations, I am contacting you at this point in the hope that we might be able to make our first contact at next month's Fine Papers International trade show. I intend to be stationed at Godfrey's kiosk throughout the show, where I hope to meet as many of my new client contacts as possible in person.

If you do attend the show I would really appreciate it if you would be kind enough to drop by Booth 417 and introduce yourself. Perhaps at that time we can take the opportunity to set up an introductory marketing familiarization meeting for the near future. Also, while you are there you will be able to enter our draw for a giant plazma wide-screen TV.

As your new Godfrey Papers Inc. Client Representative, I very much look forward to familiarizing myself with your company's operations so that I may serve you well.

I really hope that we will have an opportunity to get acquainted at the FPI show.

Yours sincerely,

Frank Samson
Client Services Unit

Voila! We have a brand new introduction letter, based on the original template - but also completely different - dealing with a totally different introduction situation.

So, as you can see from the above example, working with the real-life template, on a paragraph-by-paragraph basis, it was an easy matter to quickly adapt the approach, style and contents of the original introduction letter to create a new one to fit the new situation.

Once you get into using this method you'll find that your adapted letter will start to develop a life of its own. Soon, you'll begin adding things and you'll start plugging in your own words and phrases.

In the end you'll have a very different letter - one adapted to the specific situation for which you're writing the letter.

In most cases, your new letter will be BETTER than the template you're working from.

The important point being that; by using the Template Adaptation Method^{TM} you didn't have to start from a blank piece of paper or computer screen.

BENEFITS OF THE "TEMPLATE ADAPTATION METHOD"

The main benefits of the template adaptation approach are the following:

- Downloading the template into one's word processor and developing a new letter, paragraph-by-paragraph, saves significant time over starting from scratch.

- Using a pre-written real-life template simplifies the process of finding an approach and style for your letter.

- The template will stimulate your thinking process and will give you new ideas for your letter.

- The template will act as a "checklist" to make sure that you have covered everything you need to.

- You know that you're using a "model" that has been used successfully by others.

In short – the Template Adaptation Method^{TM} will give you a superior letter.

So, if you ever struggle with getting started writing your letters, I highly recommend that you try the Template Adaptation Method^{TM}. It will really simplify your letter-writing process.

BUSINESS-TO-BUSINESS LETTERS

This section of the manual contains 57 fully-formatted real-life templates of the most common types of letters used in day-to-day business correspondence when dealing with other businesses or institutional organizations.

For easy reference, here is a list of the categories and sample letters included in each:

Covering Letters (pg. 75)
Annual Report
Legal Documents
Progress Report

Employee Letters (pg. 79)
Award Nomination
Commendation
Condolence
Holiday Season Wishes
Job Reference
Moving Instructions
Organization Change
Promotion
Recommendation
Rejected Job Applicant
Termination, Downsizing
Unsatisfactory Performance
Unsuccessful Job Bid
Welcome New Employee
Year-End Thank You

Financial Letters (pg. 95)
Collection
Credit Approval
Credit Refusal
Credit Program Solicitation

Congratulations – Award Winner
Invitation – Conference Speaker
Justification – Laptop Computer Required
Recognition - Professional Advice
Reference – Former Customer
Thank You – Professional Assistance
Thank You – Fund-Raising Assistance

For more business-to-business letters see the Third Edition letters on page 197.

Note On Template Size

Please note that the letter templates on the following pages have been reduced in size slightly from what I consider ideal so that they could fit onto single pages of this guide. Because of this, the top and bottom margins are wider than what is recommended for a standard business letter (see pg 45). In addition, a point size of 11 has been used rather than the ideal size of 12 points.

COVERING LETTERS

A business-to-business "covering letter" is one that a company typically uses to transmit other documents such as reports, contracts, publicity, or legal documents to another company or organization. These are sometimes referred to as "transmittal letter" or "letter of transmittal".

The following pages contain some real-life templates of business-to-business covering letters.

Covering Letters

Note On Template Size

Please note that the letter templates on the following pages have been reduced in size slightly from what I consider ideal so that they could fit onto single pages of this guide. Because of this, the top and bottom margins are wider than what is recommended for a standard business letter (see pg 45). In addition, a point size of 11 has been used rather than the ideal size of 12 points.

Cover: (annual report)

(print Cover Letter for a report on business letterhead paper)

October 31, 20xx

Ms. Karen Lambton
Chief Financial Officer
Dynamic Solutions Inc.
2005 40th St.
North Bergen, NJ 07045

Dear Ms. Lambton:

Further to your telephone inquiry yesterday, enclosed is a copy of Merrick's Annual Report for the 20xx-20xx operating year.

As I mentioned, the financial results in terms of earnings per share need to be qualified as per the notes included on pages 28 and 29. As explained there, we had a number of extraordinary transactions last year which caused the earnings picture to appear understated in comparison with what we expect for this year. In fact, it is our firm expectation that this year's per share earnings figures will be twice that of last year.

With respect to the numerous questions you had regarding our publishing operations, would you please have a look at the summary of operations on pages 31 to 33. There is plenty of specific detail there that will likely answer most of your questions. If you still have questions after reviewing that information, please feel free to give me a call at 235-9867. If I can't answer your questions I will put you in touch with those who will be able to.

Thanks very much for your interest in Merrick Industries. If I don't hear from you in the meantime, I look forward to getting your feedback at the November CFO Society meeting.

Yours sincerely,

Herman Reddfield
Chief Financial Officer

Enclosure (1)

Cover: (legal documents)

(print Cover Letter for legal papers on business letterhead paper)

December 15, 20xx

Ms. Joanna Harley
Senior Counsel
Thompson, Underwood & Warwick
4305 Avenue Road, Suite 1450
Toronto, ON, M5W 1F7

Dear Joanna:

This is further to our meeting earlier this week regarding our upcoming civil action against Winstone Press regarding copyright violations. Here's a list of the enclosed documents:

- Original Copyright Certificate of Registration for "Internet Basics Without Fear!" , registration date , October 12, 20xx.

- Copy of manuscript of "Internet Basics Without Fear!" that was sent to Jason Winstone at Winstone Press on July 30, 20xx.

- Marked-up copy of Winstone Press publication entitled "Internet Basics for Beginners", showing in yellow hi-liter, all identical and almost identical passages to "Internet Basics Without Fear!.

- Invoice from Leadzone Book Printing, dated October 30, 20xx for the printing and production of 5,000 copies of "Internet Basics Without Fear!".

- Copy of Final Draft! general news release for "Internet Basics Without Fear!" dated November 15, 20xx.

- Copy of Winstone Press publicity release for their book "Internet Basics For Beginners", dated December 1, 20xx.

- Letter sent by me to Jason Winstone, dated December 5, 20xx.

I trust that these will provide you with the information that you need to pursue our action in the Courts on an urgent basis. Please let me know right away if you need anything else.

Sincerely,

Michael Varty
Final Draft! Publications Inc.

Enclosures (7)

Cover: (progress report)

(print Cover Letter for a report on business letterhead paper)

July 21, 20xx

Mr. Raymond Keefer
Director of Operations
Aircraft Manufacturing Division
Alliance Aerospace Inc.
1825 Pedrogosa Street, Suite 1200
Santa Barbara CA 93101

Dear Mr. Keefer:

Attached is the latest version of the strategic plan update and working papers. I have made all of the adjustments that you requested in your recent e-mail. In addition, I have completed the new section on "performance indicators" based on the inputs received from the branches last week.

Performance Indicators
Each directorate/branch prepared its own version of the entire matrix that John Hannon had suggested. Essentially, for the strategic plan document I took those inputs and consolidated them into one overall corporate matrix. I eliminated duplicates and redundancies and cleaned up the wording and terminology.

Strategic Plan
As mentioned, I have incorporated all of your comments. Additional changes are:
- Note re: "Working Papers" has been added to the bottom of the Preface page.
- Pages 10 through 15 are the new consolidated Performance Indicator pages.

Working Papers
Revisions to the Working Papers are:
- A brief Introduction has been added to summarize the contents.
- Pages 13 through 20 have been added. These are the Directorate/Branch submissions on Performance Indicators.

I'm not sure what you had in mind for the review process. Nevertheless, I have a suggestion. If you deem the enclosed to be in acceptable shape for review, you could send review copies to the Senior Management Committee, with a cover letter proposing a meeting at which comments could be tabled and discussed by all. Hopefully, I would be able to attend that meeting, and collect all of the comments and their final resolutions direct from the originators.

The foregoing is just a suggestion of course. Please let me know how you would like to handle the review and revision process and I will comply with whatever your wishes are. If you would like, I could draft a brief letter of transmittal to your directors, for your signature.

Sincerely,

Sam Beaubien
Senior Partner – Kaizen Consulting Inc.

Attachments (2)

EMPLOYEE LETTERS

A business-to-business "employee letter" is an internal company business letter. Typically it is a letter that a company sends to one of its employees to advise the employee of various matters related to their employment status with the company.

The following pages contain real-life templates of the most common internal business-to-business employee letters.

Please take note. Since employee letters are "internal" business letters, many of them can also be written in the form of an internal corporate memorandum. Accordingly, the following templates include examples of both letter and memo formats.

Employee Letters

Note On Template Size

Please note that the letter templates on the following pages have been reduced in size slightly from what I consider ideal so that they could fit onto single pages of this guide. Because of this, the top and bottom margins are wider than what is recommended for a standard business letter (see pg 45). In addition, a point size of 11 has been used rather than the ideal size of 12 points.

Employee: (award nomination)

(print Award Nomination Letter on corporate memo letterhead paper)

CONFIDENTIAL MEMORANDUM

Date: December 20, 20xx

From: Bill Kelly

To: John Stanton
              Executive Director

Subject: Nomination – Miranda Zellios – Jeremy Scanlan Award, 20xx

The purpose of this is to submit the name of Miranda Zellios as a nominee for the 20xx "Jeremy Scanlan Award for Excellence in Aircraft Accident Investigation."

Since July 1998 when Miranda first joined this agency, she has consistently demonstrated her superior skills, abilities, and professionalism as a member of the aviation accident investigation group. I believe she is a shining example of everything that is signified by the "Jeremy Scanlan Award", and therefore should be given the award for 20xx. I will briefly summarize the reasons for my nomination:

- Miranda was instrumental in leading a successful search and recovery effort when the Air Orion B-707 crashed into Lake Ontario in December 20xx.

- As investigator-in-charge of the Air Orion investigation, she has set a new standard for applying project management techniques to a major accident investigation.

- Miranda's performance in dealing with all parties involved has been exceptional. These parties included: next-of-kin, the media, police forces, interested parties, and other government agencies. She is clearly a gifted communicator and negotiator.

- She and her team of investigators managed to produce a comprehensive draft report for Board review within 15 months of the accident date. As you know, this is unprecedented for a major investigation and has set a new standard for this agency.

- Even though she was pre-occupied with the Air Orion investigation, Miranda managed to make significant contributions to the drafting of the Board's new "Investigation Policy".

I'm sure you will agree that Miranda's contribution has been outstanding and exemplifies the qualities of excellence and professionalism that are embodied in the Jeremy Scanlan Award.

I look forward to our discussion of the nominees at next week's Management Council Meeting.

Bill Kelly
Director, Investigation Operations

Employee: (commendation)

(print Employee Commendation Memo on corporate letterhead paper)

MEMORANDUM

Date: September 30, 20xx

From: Melody Franklin

To: Franco Marconi
          Director, Research Support Programs

Subject: <u>Commendation – Herbert Singleton – Freight Transport Demand Project</u>

The purpose of this is to officially commend Herbert Singleton for his exceptional contribution throughout his assignment to the Freight Transport Demand Project (FTDP).

As you know, Herbert has been working on special assignment with the FTDP team for the past eight months. Now that he is about to return to your part of the organization I wanted to make sure that he gets some recognition for his significant and exceptional contributions to the project.

As a junior econometrician, Herbert's role in the project was pivotal to its timely and successful completion. It was Herbert who worked long hours, numerous nights and weekends with his small team of researchers, first specifying, and then testing the thousands of equations that had to be run. The quality of Herbert's written work was also exceptional. His regression analysis summaries were always very well written and rarely required revision.

As a colleague and project team member, Herbert was also outstanding. His upbeat enthusiasm for the project was infectious, and he seemed to motivate the entire project team. He was very well-liked by all team members, and in effect he became "unofficial" deputy project manager.

In closing, I would like to say that I have worked with many junior economists and econometricians over the years and have never run across one as professional and productive as Herbert Singleton was on the FTDP. I believe that the organization as a whole should recognize his exceptional contribution to a major project.

Please let me know if you have any questions or comments.

Melody Franklin
Director, Econometric Research

cc: Herbert Singleton
     Personnel file – H. Singleton

Employee: (condolence)

(Ideally, personal Letters of Condolence should be hand-written)

175A Fairmont Ave.
Toronto, ON
M5W 1F2

August 13, 20xx

Dear Robert:

I would like to express my sincere condolences on the recent passing of your father. Pamela and the children also send their thoughts and prayers to you and your family at this difficult time.

Although I didn't know your dad that well, on the half dozen or so occasions that I spent time in his company over the years, I did come to realize his great kindness and compassion towards those less fortunate than him. And I do know that he was very highly respected throughout this community and profession, and his good works changed the lives of many.

You were truly fortunate to have such a man as a model in your life.

As you know, it was not that long ago that my own father passed away, so I have some idea of what you and your family are going through. No comfort is quite enough to replace the loss.

Please pass my deepest sympathies on to your mother, and brother, and sister, and to all of your father's grandchildren.

Very sincerely,

Gord Henderson

Employee: (holiday season wishes)

(print Holiday Season Wishes on corporate letterhead paper)

MEMORANDUM

Date: December 20, 20xx

From: Kevin Dalton
             President and CEO

To: All Winton Systems Inc. Employees

Subject: <u>Holiday Season Best Wishes To All!</u>

The holiday season gives us time to reflect on our lives and to be thankful for the many blessings that have come to us. It is also a time when we tend to become more aware of those less fortunate in our own society and in the rest of the world. Those of us who can afford to give what we can to help those in need.

The holidays also provide us with an opportunity to gather together with family and friends to celebrate and express our gratitude for their presence in our lives. At work, we socialize with our co-workers more than usual, and we work together as a team raising funds for various charitable causes. Many of us ride the spirit of the season to personally extend our best wishes to our customers and suppliers.

I truly enjoy watching each year how this season seems to bring out the very best in all of us as human beings, regardless of our personal or spiritual beliefs. For this reason, I find it a wonderful time of year.

In closing, I would like to take this opportunity on behalf of the Executive Team to wish you and your loved ones the very best of health and happiness for this holiday season and throughout the coming New Year.

Best Wishes of the Season,

Kevin Dalton

Employee: (job reference)

(print Employee Reference Letter on corporate letterhead paper)

July 15, 20xx

To Whom It May Concern:

<u>Re: Employment Reference – Randy Quirkes</u>

This is to confirm that Randy Quirkes worked under my direct supervision as an Insurance Sales Representative from January 20xx to October 20xx.

During that period Randy progressed from sales initiation trainee to fully certified sales representative by the time he left for another job.

I would say that Randy is a hard working individual who learns quickly. He is generally cooperative and can perform well as a member of a team, although he prefers to work independently. He communicates very well orally and is working hard to improve his writing skills. I saw considerable improvement in this area during the last year he was with us.

As a sales professional, Randy was always above the 50th percentile of performers on my sales team. Since he started from scratch only two years before, and most of his colleagues were highly experienced with strong, established networks, I would say that Randy achieved a lot in his early years as a sales representative.

So, based on what I observed during my two years with Randy, I believe he has excellent potential to become a high-performing sales professional in the insurance business.

For further information, I can be reached at (416) 972-0539.

Sincerely,

Dominick Creaghan
Director, Sales and Marketing Operations

Employee: (moving instructions)

(print Moving Instructions on corporate letterhead paper)

MEMORANDUM

Date: November 4, 20xx

From: Janice Sizemore
           Director, Administrative Services

To: All Employees – Quality Testing Branch -5th Floor

Subject: <u>Move To the 10th Floor – November 8-9, 20xx</u>

The move to your new offices on the 10th floor is scheduled to take place during the coming weekend.

In order for things to run smoothly during the move, you are asked to follow the guidelines below:

- Each staff member is required to clean out their own desk and pack up the contents in boxes prior to leaving the office on Friday. Boxes will be provided to you in your work area on Thursday Nov 6/06.

- You are also asked to please remove everything from the walls in your work area and also pack those items in the supplied boxes.

- Make sure that you clearly mark your first initial and last name on the top and sides of each box. You are asked to number each box in sequence and make a note of your total box count for later cross-checking that all of your material has been received.

- If you have personal belongings and/or valuables in your workspace you should take them home with you before the move. During the confusion of a move such as this, it is easy to misplace and/or lose track of things; so in the case of your personal belongings and valuables it is better to be safe than sorry.

- On Monday morning, we will be unpack and put things away as quickly as possible, after which we will all get back to work.

- Please deposit all empty boxes and other packing material next to the wall in the hallway where the elevators are located. Signs will be posted designating the exact deposit locations.

We believe that if everyone does their part and follows the designated procedures, any disruption caused by the move will be kept to a minimum. We therefore trust that there will be no negative affects on production schedules, and current deadlines will be met.

If you have any questions or special requirements please contact Ernie Gomez (ext. 2254) as soon as possible.

Thank you all for your usual cooperation.

Janice Sizemore

Employee: (organization change)

(print Employee Organization Change Letter on corporate letterhead paper)

December 5, 20xx

Claudia Morency
Senior Database Administrator
Corporate Enterprise Solutions Group
New World Dimensions Inc.
1500 Clearview Technology Park
Berkeley, CA 95435

Dear Claudia:

Re: Corporate Restructuring Changes – Your New Reporting Relationships

The purpose of this is to advise you of the recent organizational changes that have resulted from our corporate restructuring exercise, and how they will affect you.

The major change that will impact your specific position is the elimination of the separate Technical Support Groups in each of the five main divisions. These will be replaced by one central group known as the Customer Database Support Group. This new structure will be in-place immediately after the upcoming holiday season. A copy of the new organization structure is attached for your information.

Consequently, Effective January 1, 20xx your position will report directly to the new Manager, Customer Relationship Services. That position has not yet been filled, but we are expecting to make an announcement about that by late next week. For the time being your job title will remain the same. It could possibly change as the new organization is implemented, but it is too early to tell right now.

Until that date, business will continue as usual, with you reporting to Jim Bragg.

Letters similar to this one have been sent to all of your colleagues in the Enterprise Solutions Group. In addition, we will be holding weekly information sharing sessions in the corporate auditorium each Friday afternoon., beginning at 3:00 p.m. You are welcome to attend these sessions where staff will be briefed on the latest status of the restructuring implementation and will have an opportunity to raise any questions or concerns you may have. The weekly sessions will continue until such time as the new organization structure is fully implemented.

I look forward to your usual co-operation as the organization embarks on this exciting new path.

Sincerely,

Kenneth Mancini
Director, Human Resources Group

Attach. (1)

Employee: (promotion)

(print Employee Promotion Letter on corporate letterhead paper)

February 21, 20xx

Martina Mayka
291 Alvarta Ave.
Apt. 1405
Cambridge, MA 02237

Dear Martina:

This is to advise you that the Staffing Review Committee met late last week and determined that your probationary appointment as a trainee was successful and that you should therefore be appointed immediately as a Sales and Marketing Representative (full-time).

Accordingly, this is to officially inform you that effective March 1, 20xx you will be officially appointed to the position of Sales and Marketing Representative in the Customer Service Group. Your initial appointment will be for a period of 24 months. Terms and conditions of your employment are covered by the Customer Service Group Employment Agreement, a copy of which will be mailed to you shortly.

Would you please report as soon as possible to Janet Jackman, Chief of Human Resources so that the details of your appointment may be properly documented.

Congratulations Martina! I am pleased to welcome you as a full-time member of our team. Everyone here at Info-Tech Systems is looking forward to working with you in the future.

Sincerely,

Shirley Samuelson
Manager, Customer Services Group

Employee: (recommendation)

(print Recommendation Letter on company letterhead paper)

November 23, 20xx

Mr. Roberto Vargas
Manager, Marketing Services
Allied Industries Inc.
110 Riverbend Drive, Suite 1550
Stamford, CT 06907

Dear Mr. Vargas:

This is in response to your recent request for a letter of recommendation for Maria Fuentas who worked for me up until two years ago.

Maria Fuentas worked under my direct supervision at Johnson Technologies for a period of six years ending in October 20xx. During that period, I had the great pleasure of seeing her blossom from a junior marketing trainee at the beginning, into a fully functioning Marketing, Program Co-Ordinator, in her final two years with the company. That was the last position she held before moving on to a better career opportunity elsewhere.

Maria is a hard-working self-starter who invariably understands exactly what a project is all about from the outset, and how to get it done quickly and effectively. During her two years in the Marketing Co-Ordinator position, I cannot remember an instance in which she missed a major deadline. She often brought projects in below budget, and a few were even completed ahead of schedule.

Ms. Fuentas is a resourceful, creative, and solution-oriented person who was frequently able to come up with new and innovative approaches to her assigned projects. She functioned well as a team leader when required, and she also worked effectively as a team member under the direction of other team leaders.

On the interpersonal side, Maria has superior written and verbal communication skills. She gets along extremely well with staff under her supervision, as well as colleagues at her own level. She is highly respected, as both a person and a professional, by colleagues, employees, suppliers, and customers alike.

Two years ago, when Ms. Fuentas announced her resignation to take up a new position with a larger company, we were saddened to see her leave, although we wished her the greatest success in her new undertaking. Even now, two years after her departure, I can state that her presence, both as a person and as an exemplary employee, is still missed here.

In closing, as detailed above, based on my experience working with her, I can unreservedly recommend Maria Fuentas to you for any intermediate or senior marketing position. If you would like further elaboration, feel free to call me at (416) 765-4497.

Sincerely,

Roger Chisholm
Director, Marketing and Sales

Employee: (rejected job applicant - external)

(print Rejection Letter on corporate letterhead paper)

October 25, 20xx

Mr. Donald Morrison
2950 Amherst Blvd., Suite 705
Richmond, VA 23223

Dear Mr. Morrison:

Re: Head of Security, Davidson Industries Inc., Washington, D.C.

I regret to inform you that your recent application for the Head of Security position at Davidson Industries was unsuccessful.

Although you met all of the mandatory minimum qualifications for the position, the Interview Board chose a candidate with considerably more experience than you currently possess. The chairperson of the Board asked me to convey to you his thanks for your candidacy and to tell you that with a few more years of diversified experience in the field you might well have been the successful candidate.

On behalf of Davidson Industries I thank you for your interest and effort, and I wish you all the best in your future career endeavors.

Please don't hesitate to contact me at 342-9856 should you require further information.

Sincerely,

Marilyn Litwack
Senior Staffing Officer

Employee: (termination, downsizing)

(print Employee Termination Letter on corporate letterhead paper)

January 10, 20xx

Thomas Zatinski
795 Gilmour St.
Apt. 508
Ottawa, Ontario
K2B 8M5

Dear Thomas:

It is with sincere regret that I must inform you that your employment at Addison Systems Inc. will be terminated as of Friday January 31, 20xx.

As you know, the Downsizing Task Force delivered their report to the general manager in late December, 20xx. Among the task force recommendations was the elimination of all temporary and contract positions. Since you occupy a temporary position, you are automatically subject to the task force recommendations.

I would like to make it absolutely clear that in no way does your termination reflect that the company is in any way unhappy with your work performance over the past 18 months. In fact, you have been highly regarded as one of our most productive contract staffers. Unfortunately, you and the other non-permanent staff that are being let go are simply a reflection of the general economic downturn in the fiber-optics industry over the past year.

In an effort to try to reduce the impact of this termination, the company has worked out a severance arrangement that will give you one week's pay for each month you worked beyond 12 months. In your case this will amount to six (6) weeks of severance pay. In addition, your medical and dental coverage will remain in effect until the end of the severance period. You will soon receive a letter from Human Resources with all of the details on the severance package.

Thomas, given your qualifications and proven abilities, I am confident that you will be able to find another position in the relatively near future. If you would like, I would be pleased to write a recommendation letter for you, to help with your job search.

Sincerely,

Fred Shandling
Unit Manager

Employee: (unsatisfactory performance)

(print Employee Unsatisfactory Performance Letter on corporate letterhead paper)

May 20, 20xx

By Registered Courier Mail

Gerald Hugues
15450 Don Mills Road
Apartment 1507
Toronto, ON M3B 2X7

Dear Gerald:

I am sending this to your home address via registered courier mail since you have not made an appearance at work since Friday May 10, 20xx.

This letter is written with direct reference to our telephone conversation earlier today in which I urged you to return to work as soon as possible, or to provide me with medical documentation stating that you are not able to perform your duties.

Continuing on with the points I made when we met in my office on Friday, May 10, 20xx, I want to reiterate that I have been unhappy with your overall job performance for a number of months. Ever since the company was restructured and reorganized last autumn I have noted a drastic decline in the quality of your work. In addition, your behavior and general demeanor in the office has been unacceptable on a number of occasions. As you know, each time I believed your behavior to be inappropriate I had a note placed on your personnel file to that effect.

When we met on May 10th to discuss the situation, you assured me that you were going to immediately turn over a new leaf and make the necessary changes. Instead you have not shown up for work since that day. You must be well aware that your absence during this critical period when we are finalizing the Allied Dynamics proposal is jeopardizing the company's chances of gaining that important contract.

Accordingly, this is to officially advise you that unless you report to work within 24 hours of receiving this letter, your employment with this company will be terminated effective immediately. On the other hand, if you do return within 24 hours we will be pleased to sit down with you, and Employee Services staff , to discuss how we might be able to work things out.

I look forward to your immediate return to work.

Yours sincerely,

Brendan Callaghan
Group Chief, Publishing Services

Employee: (unsuccessful job bid - internal)

(print Employee Promotion Letter on corporate letterhead paper)

March 15,, 20xx

Katarina Kovalov
238 Gloucester Sreet.
Apt. 1405
Ottawa, ON
K1E 5P2

Dear Katarina:

I regret to inform you that your recent application for the position of Marketing Coordinator was unsuccessful.

If it's any consolation, the Selection Committee did rank you among the top three candidates. Your written test results were excellent, and your performance in the interview was one of the best. Although it was very close, in the end the committee decided to go with the most experienced candidate from the short list of finalists.

Accordingly, the position has been awarded to Monica Lopez from the Sales Department.

We appreciate your participation in this job competition. Based on your performance in front of the committee, we urge you to continue gaining as much diversified experience in the field of marketing as you can. Committee members noted that you have a great deal of potential, and once you have gained more experience in the field you will have many opportunities for promotion.

If you would like further details on how you fared in the competition, let me know and I would be happy to meet with you.

Sincerely,

Marilyn Collister
Manager, Human Resources

Employee: (welcome new employee)

(print Welcome Memo on corporate memo letterhead paper)

MEMORANDUM

Date: December 1, 20xx

From: Larry Charlston
            Chief Operation Officer - VLI

To: Edwina Horvath
            Director, Creative Programs

Subject: Welcome To VideoLinks Inc.

Edwina; It is with pleasure and anticipation that I welcome you to the VideoLinks Inc. team.

As you know, VLI is a relatively new start-up in the field of online video production and distribution. We believe that as one of the first entries into this market we currently enjoy early-mover advantage, and we intend to continue to leverage that competitive-edge for as long as possible.

We have asked you to join our team because we believe that you are the kind of high-energy creative innovator that is key to our company staying in front of the pack. Marsha Valeri has told me how excited she is about the video production and marketing work that you have already done while working at AVSystems, and before that, while doing your Masters at UCLA. I must say I was impressed by what she told me; it's not very often that I've heard Marsha praising someone's past work so highly.

Because we are fairly new and relatively small, we don't yet have a formal orientation program in-place. However, I have asked our Head of Administration, Emilio Sanchez, to spend as much time as needed to brief you on every aspect of VLI's organization and operations. Then, at the end of your first week here I want to sit down with you for a few hours so we can have an in-depth discussion of technology and strategy issues. In fact, when you have finished with Emilio could you please let me know so that we can set up a firm time for our session.

Again, welcome to VLI Edwina. I look forward to a long and mutually rewarding relationship.

Larry Charlston

Employee: (year-end thank you)

(print Year-End Thank You To Employees on corporate memo letterhead paper)

MEMORANDUM

Date: January 5, 20xx

From: Ross Bagnall

To: All Employees – HMC Financial

Subject: **Thanks For A Great 20xx!**

As the year comes to a close I would like to sincerely thank each and every one of the HMC team for your efforts and achievements this year.

I first want to thank all of you for your contributions in making the month of December 20xx our best month for loan closings ever! In fact, December was just the icing on the cake to the very best closings year ever since HMC was established. It truly was an awesome year for which I congratulate each one of you! I believe our achievements in 20xx are a direct result of your hard work, commitment, and dedication – and an accurate testament to the high caliber of individuals that make up the WLO team.

I look forward to 20xx with great anticipation, and I fully expect it will be another record-breaking year for this company. The planned business process reengineering initiatives will streamline our transaction flow and should make all of our business processes more robust. I fully expect that these improvements, coupled with a number of yet unannounced innovations should make 20xx another milestone year. I believe next year will mark the beginning of an ever brighter future for this company.

My recent trip to Africa has caused me to reflect on how fortunate we all are to live in such a beautiful and prosperous part of this great nation. This truly is the land of opportunity – a land in which the vast majority of us are blessed with the freedom to use all of our talents and abilities to achieve our goals and dreams.

In closing, I thank you all for your dedicated support throughout 20xx and I wish you and your loved ones a very happy, healthy and prosperous 20xx!

Yours very sincerely,

Ross Bagnall
President and CEO

FINANCIAL LETTERS

A business-to-business "financial letter" is one that a company uses to transmit financial or account related information to another company or organization. These can range from price quotations, to statements of account, to collection letters.

The following pages contain real-life templates of business-to-business financial letters.

Financial Letters

Note On Template Size

Please note that the letter templates on the following pages have been reduced in size slightly from what I consider ideal so that they could fit onto single pages of this guide. Because of this, the top and bottom margins are wider than what is recommended for a standard business letter (see pg 45). In addition, a point size of 11 has been used rather than the ideal size of 12 points.

Financial: (collection)

(print Collection Letter on corporate letterhead paper)

January 21, 20xx

Francesca Swann
Accounts Payable Manager
Enigma Design & Graphics
2340 Ashland Road
Mansfield, OH 44905
Fairbanks, MN 55021

Dear Ms. Swann:

Re: Invoice No. 4735-02, July 31, 20xx, $14, 958.73, "Printing of 5,000 Posters"

This is further to my telephone calls to you yesterday and December 20, 20xx, as well as my letter to you dated January 15, 20xx, all regarding the above-noted outstanding account.

As you know, the posters were delivered to your company on July 20, 20xx, as ordered.

Our standard terms call for payment within 30 days of delivery. However, in September 20xx, at your request, I agreed to extend that period to 90 days to help your company out with its cash flow problems. That meant that the balance owing was due on October 31, 20xx.

On both occasions that I followed-up with you by telephone, in November and December 20xx, you assured me that payment of the full outstanding amount would be forthcoming in a matter of a few days. That never happened.

That account is now almost six (6) months overdue as I write this. Of course, this is unacceptable.

I would ask you to please remit payment in full by the end of this week. If we have not received payment by that time, I will have to consult with our legal counsel to see what courses of action are open to us to recover these funds as quickly as possible.

Sincerely,

Ron Harding.
Chief, Accounts Receivable

Financial: (credit approval)

(print Credit Approval Letter on corporate letterhead paper)

April 25, 20xx

Mr. Brian Fletcher
President and CEO
How-To Publications Inc.
650 Aviation Parkway
Manhattan Beach, CA 90266

Dear Brian Fletcher:

<u>Re: Your Application For Credit With TriWay Paper Products Inc.</u>

I am pleased to inform you that your recent credit application with this company has been approved and will be fully activated on May 1, 20xx.

Following is the standard procedure for dealing with our customers with credit:

- On the first day of each month we will prepare and send you a statement of all transactions for the previous month.

- Payment in full is due within 30 days of the statement date. Overdue accounts will be charged interest at the rate of 1.5% per day against all outstanding amounts.

- If an account is not fully paid within 90 days, credit privileges will be automatically suspended, unless we have agreed to special arrangements.

I am advised that your first order of 20 boxes of book printing paper will be ready for shipment on May 5, 20xx.

We are delighted that you have chosen TriWay as your paper supplier and we look forward to a long and mutually beneficial relationship with your company.

Sincerely,

Ernesto Palumbo
Credit Manager

Financial: (credit refusal)

(print Credit Refusal Letter on corporate letterhead paper)

March 21, 20xx

Mr. Lawrence Phillips
General Manager
Arcadia Industries Inc.
110 Riverbend Drive
Stamford, CT 06905

Dear Mr. Phillips:

Re: Credit Application – Arcadia Industries Inc.

Thank you for your recent credit application and for placing an order with Dromex Textiles Inc.
We look forward to doing business with your company on an ongoing basis.

We have thoroughly researched your credit application and, unfortunately, are unable to approve it at this time. Our firm policy is that all new clients must have a minimum of five (5) clean credit references with active companies that are listed with Dunn and Bradstreet.

If you can supply three (3) more of these references we would be happy to review your application once again. If so, please send the additional references directly to me.

Our standard policy for dealing with new businesses with a limited credit history is to work with them on a cash basis for the first year, and then if all goes well during that time, negotiate a mutually agreeable credit arrangement for the future. As an incentive, we offer a 7.5% discount on all cash purchases made during that first year.

Again, I thank you on behalf of Dromex Textiles, and I wish you every success in your new business venture.

Sincerely,

Susan Dalrymple
Manager, Credit Operations

Financial: (credit program solicitation)

(print Credit Program Solicitation Letter on corporate letterhead paper)

February 7, 20xx

Ms. Sondra Drumheller
President and General Manager
Quite Right Gifting Inc.
4055 Woodland Ave.
Montreal, QC, H3C 1L2

Dear Ms. Drumheller:

In appreciation for your business over the past 18 months, we would like to invite you to take advantage of our Preferred Merchant Credit Program.

We set this program up to reward our best customers with a credit option that offers flexibility and excellent financial terms. As a Preferred Merchant, here is what you will get:

- Up to 90 days of credit financing on all purchases you make with Woodwind Novelties Inc.

- You get a full 30 days after the invoice date to pay with no interest fees applicable.

- From 30 to 60 days, we offer a low interest rate of just 1% per month on all outstanding balances.

- Extensions beyond 90 days will be considered under special circumstances with an interest rate of 1.5%.

- Total credit purchases accumulated during each quarter will qualify you for discounts in the following quarter based on a percentage of the total purchases made in the previous period.

We hope you will accept our offer and become a Woodwinds Preferred Merchant. To apply, please fill out the brief questionnaire that is attached to this and then send it to me.

Sincerely,

Jeffrey Archer
Manager, Preferred Customer Program

Attach. (1)

Financial: (invoice)

(print Invoice Letter on business letterhead paper)

<u>INVOICE 02-034</u>

To: **Eric MacBride**   **From:** **Sharon Foster**
Editor – ICAA Digest   (as per above)
ICAA
999 University St., Ste. 1205
Montreal, QC, H3C 5H7

Fax	(516) 954-6376	Pages:	1

Phone:	(516) 954-8222	Date:	**Nov. 19, 20xx**
Re:	**Somalia Article for ICAA Digest – Research and Writing**	CC:	

Please regard this as an INVOICE for English editorial services provided while researching and writing a feature article re: the Somalia Caretaker Authority Project for publication in the December 20xx ICAA Quarterly Digest Magazine. Work was performed Nov. 12-18/02. Final copy (3,800 words) submitted to Client by e-mail on Nov. 18/02.

English Editorial Services	30.0 hours	at $ 60.00 per hr.	=	$	1,800.00
GSTax at 7.0% (142687426) `					126.00
QSTax at 7.5% (101394564)					144.45

TOTAL Amount Owing (payable <u>within 30 days</u> of Invoice date)   =   **$ 2,070.45**

Thanks very much for this work. Please don't hesitate to contact me should you have a requirement for editorial or consulting services in the future.

Sincerely,

Sharon Foster

Financial: (letter of credit)

(print Letter of Credit on corporate letterhead paper)

July 1, 20xx

City of West Waterford
Community Development Department
Engineering Branch
1310 New Capital Avenue
West Waterford, CA, 95593

Subject: Letter of Credit - Jackson Bros. Construction Inc.
          Project A-045-595 - Upgrade/Repave Parking Lot

To Whom It May Concern:

Please be advised that we have placed a hold on the line of credit of Jackson Brothers Construction Inc. in the amount of $650,000 for the benefit of the City of West Waterford for the work related to the above-noted public improvement project.

This hold is effective July 1, 20xx and will remain in effect until the work is completed and approved by the City of West Waterford.

Chambers Bank will secure said funds as a guarantee to the City of West Waterford for completion of the named public improvements in accordance with City permits.

Funds guaranteed by said line of credit will only be restored to Jackson Brothers Construction Inc. after Chambers Bank has received written confirmation from the Director of Community Development of the City of West Waterford that said improvements have been satisfactorily completed in accordance with the approved construction permit.

Chambers Bank agrees to disperse funds from the line of credit to the City of West Waterford upon written demand of the Director of Community Development, accompanied by the statement that conditions of the construction permit have been violated.

This is an irrevocable commitment of funds which is not subject to recall by Jackson Brothers Construction Inc.

Sincerely,

_____
John Livingstone
Corporate Credit Department

We Concur with this agreement:

_____
Fred Jackson
President

Financial: (price quotation)

(print Price Quotation Letter on corporate letterhead paper)

January 26, 20xx

Rosalind Turner
Classic Graphics Inc.
1395 Cannon Circle
Fairbanks, MN 55021

Dear Rosalind:

Re: "The Self-Destructive Use of Drugs" – Mini-Poster Flyers

Further to our phone conversation a couple of days ago, enclosed are 25 sample "mini-poster flyers" for you to use in promoting the poster to some of your customers. We developed it so that it would have the same look and feel as the large poster.

Consequently, it is a 4-color, heavy-duty, double-laminated replica of the actual poster. We needed something that we could mail to prospective customers where we thought that mailing the full-sized poster as a sample would be a bit too much. As I told you on the phone, we only send the full-size poster when we are talking seriously to a customer about a quantity purchase.

Normally, we sell the generic version of these "mini-poster flyers" to our distributors at USD$1.50 each. Typically, they order 100 or less at a time. We are able to offer this special low price because we had a large quantity of the generic version printed in one run. If we were to print a small quantity, such as 100 mini-posters in one run, our unit cost would be almost double the $1.50 figure that we now charge for a single flyer. The primary reason for this is high set-up costs for the lamination process when volumes are lower.

We have developed a special price schedule for Classic Graphics should you be interested in using this flyer for your own marketing purposes, as follows:

Quantity	IDARP Generic Version (USD$ per unit)	Custom Logo Version (USD$ per unit)
100	1.50	2.30
500	1.50	1.60
1,000	1.20	1.20
5,000	0.60	0.60

The above prices do not include shipping, which would be billed to you directly by the shipper.

Please let us know if you would like to order additional copies of the "mini-poster flyer." As usual, I can be reached at 1-800-605-6750. My Fax is (819) 989-7643, and my e-mail is ronz@idarp.com.

Sincerely,

Ron Zamboni.
Director, Sales and Marketing

Enclosures (25)

INTRODUCTION LETTERS

An "introduction letter" or "letter of introduction" is one that a company normally uses to introduce itself, or one of its representatives, to another company or organization.

The following pages contain some real-life templates of business-to-business introduction letters.

Introduction Letters

Note On Template Size

Please note that the letter templates on the following pages have been reduced in size slightly from what I consider ideal so that they could fit onto single pages of this guide. Because of this, the top and bottom margins are wider than what is recommended for a standard business letter (see pg 45). In addition, a point size of 11 has been used rather than the ideal size of 12 points.

Introduction: (business associate)

(print Introduction Letters on corporate letterhead paper)

April 13, 20xx

Ms. Manuela Fernandez
Senior Partner
New Vistas Consulting Inc.
1110 Beacon Street, Suite 3500
Boston, MA 02108

Dear Manuela:

The bearer of this letter is Roberta Olson, the person I spoke to you about on the phone last week. As I explained then, Roberta is moving back to the east coast next month for personal reasons.

I would very much appreciate it if you could spare a few hours to get to know Roberta. If you do, our loss here at McMeaghan and Partners could well be your gain at New Vistas.

Roberta has been one of our top management consultants for the past five years. During that time she has taken on some difficult assignments and has consistently achieved outstanding results. She has become our top expert on Customer Relationship Management (CRM) and has been asked to speak on the subject frequently. She has also published a number of oft-quoted papers on that subject as well.

Roberta has demonstrated a strong leaning towards one-to-one marketing ever since we participated in the Executive MBA program together at Kellogg in the early 1990s.

If you have any clients that are interested in developing a one-to-one CRM strategy, Roberta would be the perfect expert to work with you.

In any case, I'll let you draw your own impression of Roberta when you meet with her. As you suggested, I have asked her to call you and arrange a meeting as soon as she gets settled in Boston.

It was great talking to you last week Manuela. It took me back too the "good old days" at Kellogg. Please give me a call so we can get together the next time you come to Seattle.

All the best,

Charles Meredith
Managing Partner

Introduction: (former employee)

(print Introduction Letter on corporate letterhead paper)

August 12, 20xx

Ms. Judith Baxter
Senior Buyer
Avon Books & Things
125 Fifth Ave., Suite 1540
New York, NY 10010

Dear Judith:

I would like to take this opportunity to introduce APN Sales Representative, Peter Lenester, whom I spoke to you about recently.

As I mentioned on the phone, Peter spent the last eight years with APN Publishing House as both a Book Buyer and then a Regional Sales Rep. He was very successful in both of these jobs and managed to learn a great deal about the book publishing business along the way.

As I also mentioned when we spoke, Peter is moving back to New York for family reasons. One of his children suffers from a rare blood disorder. The Columbia University Medical Center is the leading research institute looking into that disease and they have agreed to accept Peter's son as a special study patient.

We will be very sorry to see Peter leave the company. He has proven to be a valuable asset in dealing with our existing clients, and in recruiting new ones. The fact that he has a degree in English Literature from New York University, coupled with him being a self-published author, gives him a great deal of credibility when dealing with these people.

If you could spare a couple of hours to meet with Peter I have no doubt that the two of you would very quickly find a lot of common ground. He's the kind of person who, once you get to know him, you want to make room for him.

Judith, I thank you in advance for taking the time to meet with Peter and I look forward to visiting with you at next month's homecoming gathering at our alma mater.

Sincerely,

Amy Winston
Publisher

Introduction: (professional facilitation)

(print Introduction Letter on corporate letterhead paper)

July 27, 20xx

Professor Andrew Morrissey
Executive Director
Executive MBA Program
University of Ottawa
350 O'Connor St., Suite 350
Ottawa, ON, K1P 1A4

Dear Professor Morrissey:

Please allow me to introduce the bearer of this letter, Ms. Catherine Nasslund. Catherine is the architect that I spoke to you about last week when we talked on the phone.

As I explained, I am working on a feasibility study for one of the university programs here in Montreal that is considering the development of an Executive Management Training Centre. Part of my study involves having to estimate the possible fit-up costs for the proposed new centre.

The client is intent on making sure they get a "state-of-the-art" executive training facility. Naturally I thought of my alma mater at the Ottawa U. Executive MBA center, as the perfect example as to how it's done.

As we discussed, if you would be kind enough to have one of the staff members there spend about one hour giving Catherine a tour of the facilities there, I would very much appreciate it. Catherine tells me that it is important that she take the tour when the classroom and case rooms will not be in use, since she will need to take various measurements.

As you suggested, Catherine contacted Sharon Hudson of your staff to make sure that she would be traveling there at a time when it would be possible to do everything she needs to do.

Thanks so much Professor Morrissey. I really appreciate your co-operation on this.

All the best,

David Carruthers, M.B.A.
Senior Consultant

Introduction: (self-introduction - sales)

(print Introduction Letter on corporate letterhead paper)

August 12, 20xx

Mr. Brent Collinson
Senior Buyer
Office-Tech Furnishings Inc.
4830 Kimbark Ave.
Chicago, IL 60635

Dear Mr. Collinson:

The purpose of this letter is to briefly introduce myself as Dynatek's new Sales Representative, Business Accounts. I very recently joined the company and am taking over your account from Jack Winters who has moved on to other challenges in this industry.

I have just completed Dynatek's management orientation program and am now keen to meet face-to-face with all of my key customers.

Accordingly, as a first step in my customer familiarization process, I would like to meet with you personally, for about an hour or so, to discuss Office-Tech's needs and concerns. At the same time I would also like to take that opportunity to briefly review Dynatek's latest offering of products and services.

To set up a meeting for this at your convenience, I propose to call your office by the end of this week. It is my hope that we will be able to arrange to meet at your offices before the end of the month.

As your new Dynatek Business Account Representative I believe that my paramount concern is how both Dynatek Inc. and I can better serve Office-Tech Furnishings Inc.

I look forward to meeting with you and learning more about your company in the near future.

Sincerely,

Jim O'Malley
Senior Sales Representative

Introduction: (self-introduction - service)

(print Introduction Letter on corporate letterhead paper)

August 27, 20xx

Address List Line 1
Address List Line 2
Address List Line 3

Dear [Doctor's Name]:

"Healing Touch" Massage Therapy

My name is Anne Preston and I would like to take this opportunity to briefly introduce myself as a new member of the Danforth and area health and wellness community.

I am a Registered Massage Therapist and a graduate of the American College of Massage and Hydrotherapy. I have more than 10 years experience as a practicing Massage Therapist and have taken numerous courses in addition to my original basic training. My primary areas of interest are:

- **Pregnancy Massage**
- **Sports Therapy**
- **Craniosacral Therapy**

Research conducted by the Touch Research Institute (TRI) which is associated with the University of Miami School of Medicine, has resulted in more than 50 published studies that confirm the benefits of massage therapy, at all stages of life, from newborns to senior citizens. (www.miami.edu/touch-research). Those studies concluded that many of today's health problems can be alleviated through Massage Therapy because manipulation of soft tissues affects so many bodily systems. Benefits of Massage Therapy revealed in that research include:

CHRONIC FATIGUE AND FIBROMYALGIA
Massage Therapy recipients showed improved sleep patterns, decreased pain and depression, reduced levels of anxiety, and lower corticol stress hormones.

MIGRAINE HEADACHES
Massage Therapy decreased the occurrence of headaches, sleep disturbances and distress symptoms.

PREGNANCY
Massage Therapy during pregnancy resulted in decreased anxiety and stress hormones, and fewer obstetric and postnatal complications, including lower prematurity rates.

Massage Treatments primarily aims to:

- Improve circulation
- Reduce overall stress levels
- Improve immune system function
- Reduce tension in muscles

If you think that any of your patients could benefit from Massage Therapy I would be pleased to discuss any questions or concerns you may have. Please feel free to call me at 735-6779. I would welcome the opportunity to become a part of your health and wellness team.

Yours in good health,

Anne Preston M.T.

MARKETING AND PUBLICITY LETTERS

A business-to-business "publicity letter" is one that a company uses to make industry announcements or to promote its products or services throughout the industry marketplace in which it operates. Typical publicity letters would include new product announcements and announcements of senior executive appointments.

The following pages contain some real-life templates of business-to-business publicity letters.

Marketing and Publicity Letters

Note On Template Size

Please note that the letter templates on the following pages have been reduced in size slightly from what I consider ideal so that they could fit onto single pages of this guide. Because of this, the top and bottom margins are wider than what is recommended for a standard business letter (see pg 45). In addition, a point size of 11 has been used rather than the ideal size of 12 points.

Publicity: (corporate news release)

(print News Release on corporate letterhead paper)

FOR IMMEDIATE RELEASE

BATT-TECH Productions Inc. Takes A New Name – Will Now Be Known As ACROBAT Corporation

(Montreal, September 30, 20xx) - Batt-Tech Productions Inc. is changing its corporate name to ACROBAT Corporation. The change takes effect September 30, 20xx.

Batt-Tech, a wholly-owned subsidiary of Hydro-Alliance, was established in 1994 to conduct pilot plant activities related to the development of the lithium-nickel-polymer (LNP) battery. Prior to Batt-Tech, Hydro-Alliance's research institute had been conducting research and development into LNP technology since 1979.

The new name is another step in the company's plan to manufacture and commercialize its world-leading LNP battery technology on a global basis. The re-naming follows the assembly of a new senior management team during the past year. That experienced and market-savvy team was chosen to lead the company as it prepares to launch its LNP battery products in the global marketplace over the next few years. The first two industries targeted as potential major users of LNP batteries are the telecommunications stationary power sector and the automotive electric vehicles sector.

"Adopting a new name is just a natural evolvement for us as we fast-track our unique LNP technology to the marketplace", stated Boris Cadet, President and Chief Executive Officer. He added, "The old name served the company very well during the pilot program days and we will all be a little sad to leave it behind, but it is now time for us to adopt a new image that will get us noticed in the global battery marketplace."

Along with the new name, ACROBAT has embraced an entirely new corporate look, with a stylized logo, as well as new company colors, both of which will define its new corporate signature on all company documents and give it a distinctive identity in the marketplace.

ACROBAT Corporation is the world leader in the development of lithium-nickel-polymer battery technology. LNP technology is widely recognized as the foremost in advanced solid-state battery design. ACROBAT is currently perfecting its LNP batteries for use in stationary applications (telecommunications) and in both HEVs (hybrid electric vehicles) and EVs (pure electric vehicles). Based just outside of Montreal, Canada, ACROBAT plans to launch its automotive line of batteries by 20xx, following a launch in the telecommunications sector in 20xx.

- 30 -

Information:
Pierre Colombe or France St-Michel, ACROBAT (450) 455-3262, colombep@acrobat.com
David Dresden , DD Communications, (514) 327-8205, dresden@videotron.ca

Sales: (mail-out - direct industry)

(print Sales Letter on corporate letterhead)

August 28, 20xx

Ms. Margarita Gonzalez
Acquistions Manager
Infinity Publications Inc.
855 Duran Av., Suite 780
Pacifica, CA, 94044

Dear Ms. Gonzalez:

<u>**A Different Kind of Internet Book!**</u>

I am writing to you because your company has been recommended as one of the top book distributors in the United States for moving books into the traditional book buying market. We believe that we have a unique product for those stores and therefore, before going to reprint, I would like to check with you to see if you are interested in ordering a quantity on consignment for sale in the stores of your clients.

Enclosed for your review, is a copy of ***Internet Basics without fear! Quick-Start Guide for Becoming Internet-Friendly In Just a Few Easy Steps.*** With it, you will find a promotional brochure and a couple of recent reviews. As the information states, this is <u>an Internet book with a big difference</u>. Rather than the typical 300 plus page tekkie-type manuals that proliferate the market these days ("Dummies" books included!), it is a 100+ page people-friendly book, designed to help ordinary people become familiar with, and get connected to the Net.

The cover tells the whole story in a snapshot and was designed to quickly attract the attention of its intended target audience. As you can see, it has a very colorful and catchy design with a clear message that is perfect for attracting potential buyers. And of course as you are most surely aware, the subject of the Internet is a very hot one these days! I have no doubt that such a basic people-friendly book would appeal to many shoppers if strategically placed in the stores of your clients. In addition to personal use, this book could also be purchased as a gift for family, friends and relatives. The low price point of $11.95 makes it an attractive impulse and/or gift buy.

Our research to-date has indicated that there is a sizable niche market out there for a book just like this. Early market tests have confirmed this. People seem to be thrilled with the idea of such a basic user-friendly approach to help them get onto the Net. The book is written in clear, concise English, with a minimum of technical jargon. It also takes a human approach by discussing and dealing with the "fear of technology" issue before plunging into the "how-to" part.

Remember, between 50% and 60% of the North American market are not yet online and many are now clamoring to get connected. <u>**This book is the vehicle to help the ordinary person get there.**</u>

Thank you for your consideration and we look forward to hearing from you soon.

Sincerely,

Robert Christian
Marketing Manager

Enclosures (3)

Sales: (mail-out - targeted businesses)

(print Sales Letter on corporate letterhead)

August 28, 20xx

Mr. Ricardo Hession
President and CEO
Network Solutions Inc.
1253 Centrepointe Place
Calgary, AB, T5J 4C1

Dear Mr. Hession:

You are one of a few select Calgary business executives that we have chosen to advise about our exclusive limousine services. Accordingly, we respectfully ask you to kindly give this one-page letter your brief attention so that we can convey a special introductory offer to you.

First, let us tell you about A1 Airport Limousine Services. We have been operating an executive limousine service in the Calgary area for over five years. We started with three cars, and have built-up our fleet to over 20 high-end luxury vehicles. We offer the following services:

- Luxury business class, private road transportation – anywhere in the Calgary region;
- A fleet of over 20 Ford Lincoln Town Cars – all of them are Model Year – 20xx;
- Professional, multilingual, uniformed drivers – many with backgrounds in security services.

In addition to Corporate Business Class Transportation, we also provide Special Transportation Services including sight seeing city tours, and transportation for special events and weddings. These special services might be of interest to your company or its guests from out of town, or even to your own family and friends (we give "family outing discounts" on weekends).

Since we started, we have built-up an impressive corporate client list, including:

- The Government of Alberta
- The Government of Canada
- Numerous prominent law firms

Since your company is new to our service, we would like to take this opportunity to make to you a special introductory offer of 10% off of every $500 in business that your company places with us. This special good will discount is in addition to our already extremely competitive rates.

We thank you for your time and attention. We sincerely hope that you will seriously consider using A1's limousine services so that your company may take advantage of our special offer.

For more information on our services and/or rates, please don't hesitate to have your staff contact me at 488-5887, or by e-mail at airport-limo@netcom.net.

Yours very sincerely,

Tony Americus
President

Sales: (meeting follow-up)

(print Sales Letter on corporate letterhead)

April 27, 20xx

Ms. Margaret Campion
Director, Corporate Services
Riviera Industries Inc.
245 Dearborn Park Road
Chicago, Il 60610

Dear Ms. Campion:

It was a pleasure meeting you briefly at last week's Board of Trade event. It's amazing how small the world does seem sometimes, considering that we both earned our undergraduate degrees at U. of Kansas, even overlapping for one year! I suppose we were destined to eventually meet face-to-face.

I was fascinated by your synopsis of the history of Riviera Industries over the past, almost half-century. Clearly, your company has a rich corporate heritage and tradition. At the same time, the company has been blessed with a continuum of leaders of foresight and imagination who had the courage to change course at key points along the way so that the company could remain competitive and continue to lead its industry.

As I was mentioning to you, Final Edition Publications is a specialty publisher that focuses on corporate publications including annual reports, corporate profiles and corporate histories. We have been in business for over 15 years and during that time have grown from a two-person start-up, to a serious corporate publisher with over 100 employees. We have been contracted by over a dozen Fortune 500 companies to produce both annual and special occasion publications on their behalf.

After our chat at last week's meeting, it occurred to me that with Riviera approaching its 50th anniversary, it would be the perfect occasion to produce a Corporate History to celebrate your company's first half-century. It so happens, that these are exactly the types of corporate publications that we specialize in here at Final Edition. In fact, we have produced corporate histories for a number of companies.

With Riviera's 50th just around the corner, I'm sure that you have been thinking about ways to make that anniversary a special one. Accordingly, I would very much like to meet with you and show you some of the corporate work we have done, and brief you further on our services. I have a strong feeling that what we offer at Final Edition might be just the kind of thing you've been looking for to celebrate Riviera's 50th.

Please feel free to call me at 745-2398 so that we can discuss this further. If I don't hear from you by the end of next week I will follow up with you and see if we can set up a meeting at your convenience.

Yours truly,

Raymond Gaudet
Manager, Corporate Programs

Marketing: (post-conference follow-up)

(print Marketing Follow-Up Letter on corporate letterhead paper)

June 14, 20xx

Colin Bissell
Manager of Membership Services
Anti-Drug Association of America
1908 North Battle Street, Suite 1500
Alexandria, VA 22314

Dear Colin:

It was great meeting you and getting to know a little bit about both you and ADAA at last week's NASADAD Conference in Reno. I trust that your return journey went well and that you are settled back into the office routine (If such a thing is possible these days!). Although there were a few problems associated with weak traffic flow at times, overall I was satisfied with our participation as an exhibitor since I was nevertheless able to make quite a few quality contacts.

As I said last week, when I first came across the ADAA Website a few months ago I definitely saw a fit between *"The Self-Destructive Use of Drugs"* and AADA's mission to *"... build safe, healthy and drug-free communities"*. In particular, I could very clearly see the poster being used as a marketing vehicle by your organization, and also by your members. Not only does it convey a powerful and attention-grabbing anti-drug message, but with AADA's logo custom imprinted on the bottom-center, it would definitely give your organization high profile visibility throughout your communities. As I assured you, once an organization has a copy of this striking wall-hanging, it always gets hung in a prominent place.

At IDARI we truly believe that the message of *"The Self-Destructive Use of Drugs"* will have a significant impact on reducing drug-abuse once it is hanging on thousands of walls throughout North America. Its powerful and compelling depiction of the *"mind-body-drug connection,"* involving all of the major drug groups, all in one place, is unique. Can you imagine the impact that this poster will have once it is hung on the walls of every school, home, community center, government building, hospital, police station, clubhouse, lunch room, medical clinic, sports facility, doctor's office, dentist's office, military barracks, library, etc., across this continent?

As for pricing; we would be happy to put together a custom quote for you once we know the exact specifications of your order, in terms of artwork and, most importantly, quantity. Please let me know what parameters you are considering and we will be happy to do a quotation for you.

Colin, I truly hope that AADA and IDARI will be able to work together to spread the anti-drug message of *"The Self-Destructive Use of Drugs"* throughout communities across America. Please drop me a line or give me a call when you would like us to prepare a quotation for you. I can be reached in Montreal at (514) 972-2019, or at info@idari.org.

Sincerely,

Tom Zachary
Vice-President, Marketing and Communications

Publicity: (product news release)

(print News Release on corporate letterhead paper)

FOR IMMEDIATE RELEASE

Finally, A Book that Addresses the Human Side of Becoming an Internet User... *"Internet Basics without fear"*

(Montreal, January 14, 20xx) – Did you ever check out the Internet section of your local bookstore trying to find a true "beginners" book that was less than 250 pages and not packed with more technical sounding "cyber-babble" than you ever wanted to deal with? Not easy to find. Instead, you probably ended-up opening one of those intimidating volumes just to see. Immediately your heartbeat quickened, your palms got all sweaty, and your eyes glazed over as hundreds of technical terms and complicated techno-jargon suddenly leaped off the page at you. Well, you're not alone, according to Shaun Fawcett the author of a brand new Internet guide for beginners called "Internet Basics without fear!".

Fawcett asserts that although we're inundated these days with information and hype about getting connected to the Internet, a significant number of people are still avoiding the Net due to their basic fear of the technology involved. Says Fawcett, " Many people are even more fearful and alienated than they normally would be since they are surrounded by media, friends and family telling them incessantly that the Internet is a cinch for anyone. What the so-called experts don't understand is that most non-technical people are intimidated by any type of new technology. Telling them that it is easy and that they should 'get with it' on their own, just makes the fear and anxiety worse." Fawcett goes on to say, "… and then to add insult to injury, they go down to the local bookstore and find these so-called 'beginner books for imbeciles', or whatever they're called, and these tomes weigh-in at over 350 pages just brimming with overwhelming amounts of "techno-babble!"

Unlike other Internet beginner books, *"Internet Basics without fear! – Quick-Start Guide for Becoming Internet-Friendly In Just a Few Easy Steps"* does not jump straight into the technical jargon. First, the author shares the fears and misgivings that he personally experienced on his way to becoming Internet-savvy, and how he gradually overcame them. After dealing with the "fear of technology" issues, the core of the book then provides a simple eight-step approach to becoming Internet-friendly that focuses primarily on how to "surf" the Net, and send and receive E-mails. It is filled with tips, tricks, and information designed to give readers a taste for the diversity of the World Wide Web. The guide also addresses a variety of frequently asked Internet-related questions, is fully indexed for easy reference. Billed on the cover as a "non-technical book for non-technical people", it is written in plain non-technical English and is quite manageable at slightly over 130 pages in length.

A former computer programmer, Fawcett now calls himself as a "recovering-tekkie". Now a business consultant and marketing specialist, he says he wrote the book because he believes that there is a need to demystify the Internet for non-technical people. "I wanted to provide a non-intimidating step-by-step approach to getting online for those people who may be fearful of, or alienated by, the technology as I was a few years ago in my early Internet days.", he states. He points out that the book is written to be suitable for any Internet beginner, although he had seniors, homemakers and young non-technical women and men, particularly in mind.

"Internet Basics without fear!" will be officially published on January 30, 20xx and should be available in book stores by late February. To obtain advance copies call Final Draft Publications, toll-free at 1-800-650-6500.

- 30 -

Information:
Robert Christian: (514) 989-7438

Promotion: (show - trade show)

(print Promotional Letters on product or corporate letterhead paper)

October 30,20xx

To all Editors and Publishers,

Come and See a Snapshot of our Latest Products!

Genoptik Laser Photo and its network of dealers in the United States, cordially invite you to drop by our booth at PhotoPlus East for a close-up look at our latest technological breakthroughs in digital camera technology.

eyesight twilight™ - Just released in September, this is the first digital camera product that enables presentation of multiple exposures with a reliable preview image. Before this innovation it was impossible to overlay a second exposure over another digital image. With *twilight*™ it is now possible to overlay several images and display the resulting montage in preview mode before the final exposure is made.

eyesight winder™ - Also just released, this digital camera software is specially designed for the capture and processing of either moving objects or still portraits. It allows the shooting and capture of multiple images in sequence, at a speed of approximately one image per second for later review. Using *winder*™ the photographer can later view all of the memory-stored images one shot at a time, in "digital contact sheet" format, on a color computer monitor.

These leading-edge software modules are just the latest additions to Genoptik's line-up of products that make its *eyesight*™ *Digital Camera System.* a world leader They are available to all users of the *eyesight*™ system whether they work in a PC or a Macintosh based environment.

2,0XX good reasons to check us out!

Genoptik Laser Photo manufactured its 2,0XXth digital camera in 20xx. These cameras are used by professionals worldwide in the fields of: photography, prepress, archiving and, microscopy. The basis of this technology is the ProgPic 4000 family of cameras that have evolved over the past decade. In 1994, the ProgPic 4018 camera won the internationally recognized Seybold Award as best digital camera for professional use.

The longevity of Genoptik Digital Camera Systems is legendary throughout the industry. All new hardware and software developments made over the years have been designed compatible with the original base products so that users of the very first modules are able to work with the latest technological advances without changing their equipment.

Come and scan our products at Booth 929 and we will also give you an insider's look at our latest innovation, a revolutionary new Electronically Controlled Lens System.

Here's hoping to see you at PhotoPlus East!

Victor Muehlen
Marketing Director, Genoptic Products

Promotion: (show - consumer show)

(print Promotional Letters on product or corporate letterhead paper)

September 12, 20xx

[Exhibitor Address Line 1]
[Exhibitor Address Line 2]
[Exhibitor Address Line 3]

Dear [Name of Exhibitor]:

National Exhibits, Inc. invites you to San Diego's year-end closing Home & Garden Show at the Glenvale Civic Center on November 28th, 29th & 30th of 20xx.

We are working very closely with the Glenvale City Council and the Glenvale Chamber of Commerce to ensure that this show will be a huge success. The historic Glenvale Civic Center is strategically located in the heart of Glenvale, the third largest city in Los Angeles County and the third largest financial center in California. For over 60 years it has been the largest exhibit hall catering to the cities of Glenvale, Burbank, La Canada and the San Fernando Valley.

For almost a decade, local homeowners have frequented home shows in distant locations to meet their home and garden remodeling needs. Bringing a home and garden show to Glenvale will allow homeowners to conveniently meet their needs in these areas.

Please take note that this will be the very last show of the year. It will be your final chance to boost your sales and make those all-important contacts before year-end. Participating in this final show on the calendar will be a great way for you to end the year on a high note and approach the new year in a positive mindset. **So, make sure that you don't miss the November 1, 20xx final deadline to register as an Exhibitor**!

The City of Glenvale provides the ideal setting for a successful home and garden show, and we would like to invite you to share in our success. With the help of our strategic partners, our extensive marketing will reach millions of people and deliver thousands of qualified customers. We at National Exhibits can provide the kind of exposure that your company just can't afford on its own. Call and reserve your exhibit space today and ensure your company's success.

Please note that all previous National Exhibits exhibitors will be given the opportunity to re-book their original booth space up to October 1st, 20xx. After this date all spaces will be released.

Please hurry and contact us today. Exhibit space is limited and they are selling-out fast!

Once again, we thank you for your business and we are looking forward to a long and prosperous relationship.

We look forward to having you with us.

Sincerely,

Belinda Lauriano
VP Sales & Marketing

PROJECT LETTERS

A business-to-business "project letter" is one that a company uses to transmit project-related information to another company or organization. Typical project letters would include project status reports, proposal letters and cost estimates.

The following pages contain real-life templates of business-to-business project letters.

Project Letters

Note On Template Size

Please note that the letter templates on the following pages have been reduced in size slightly from what I consider ideal so that they could fit onto single pages of this guide. Because of this, the top and bottom margins are wider than what is recommended for a standard business letter (see pg 45). In addition, a point size of 11 has been used rather than the ideal size of 12 points.

Project: (letter of interest)

(print Letter of Interest for project participation on corporate letterhead)

November 18, 20xx

Mr. Raymond Fielding
President
Campus Renaissance Inc.
1850 Highridge Road
Columbus, Ohio 43201

Dear Raymond:

RE: Letter of Interest – Campus Renaissance Project

Mitchell-Maxwell and Timberline Properties are pleased to submit herewith our letter of interest to participate in your campus neighborhood redevelopment project. Attached is our preliminary proposal.

Since being invited to address this exciting opportunity, our team members have collaborated to produce a preliminary plan that we believe will energize the neighborhood, strengthen the University community, and produce long-term benefits for the entire City of Columbus.

As you know, we are a team of professionals with a proven track record in this region with the ability to successfully transform our plan into reality. Our team is comprised of members who have worked together on numerous successful projects. They have been assembled for this project because of the enormous trust and confidence thay have in one another. You can be assured that the lead partners in our group will manage the project closely and carefully, and accountability for results will never be delegated.

In the weeks ahead, we look forward to receiving comments from Campus Renaissance and the community at large about our preliminary proposal during the public consultation process. We understand that right now the plan is clearly a 'work in progress' which can only be improved by input from the various stakeholders who care the most about the area in question. We therefore look forward to using their input to develop a comprehensive integrated final development plan.

Thank you for giving us the opportunity to participate.

Sincerely,

_____
Mary Louise Lasser
Timberline Properties

_____
Roy Gooding
Mitchell-Maxwell

Attach.

Project: (meeting summary)

(print Project Meeting Summary Letter on corporate letterhead paper)

July 25, 20xx

Mr. Randall Whiting
Manager, Customer Services
Inter-Tech Solutions Inc.
2545 Lantana Ave..
Washington, D.C. 20260

Dear Randall:

This is further to our meeting of last week at which we agreed to hold a series of meetings over the next two months to review your experiences and results during the pilot implementation of the 1to1 Customer Relationship Management (CRM) program.

As discussed at that meeting, the objectives of our review sessions will be to:

- Review and assess the overall effectiveness of the program;

- Identify and document strengths weaknesses of the program;

- Propose customer-focused solutions that will address each area of weakness;

- Develop an approach and action plan for Phase 2 of the project;

- Determine the staff from each of our organizations who will be on the Phase 2 Team.

The meetings will be held every second Tuesday from 9:00 a.m. until noon, and the location will alternate between our two offices, the first one to be convened here at the Consultek office on August 19, 20xx.

As agreed, Fred Johnson of your CRM group is to act as the meeting co-ordinator and recording secretary throughout the process. At the end of the process, Deborah Buxton of Consultek (in consultation with Fred) will draft the summary report for review by the Steering Committee. As you requested, a copy of her c.v. has been enclosed.

I trust this covers all of the points that we discussed. If you have any questions or would like to add anything please give me a call at 235-5347.

We look forward to seeing you at the August 19th meeting.

Sincerely,

Cynthia Howell
Senior Consultant

Encl. (1)

Project: (status report)

(print Project Status Letter on corporate letterhead paper)

November 3, 20xx

Mr. David Hamilton
Airport General Manager
Ontario International Airport
200 Airport Parkway
Ottawa, ON, K1V 8B3

Dear David:

Re: ATB Expansion Project – Monthly Status Report – October 20xx

The overall project is progressing well and is on schedule for full commissioning in May, 20xx.

Air Terminal Building
All drawings for the new ATB have been approved and excavations commenced last week to the west of the existing terminal building. A construction office has been erected adjacent to Parking Garage No. 2. The project team will move into that facility next week.

Resurfacing of Runway 11/29
This project is now 95% complete. Final inspection is now underway. The runway should be open on a fulltime basis by November 15th.

Main Access Road to ATB
All pavement stripping operations will be completed this week and the resurfacing will get underway next week. The entire job, including inspections and fix-ups will be done by November 30th as per the project schedule. As you know, we are phasing the pavement work so as to minimize disruption to traffic.

New Air Cargo Terminal
The contractor has just completed the footings and will begin installation of the structural steel shortly. As per the project schedule, the plan is to have this building totally closed-in before the snow flies. This target appears achievable.

Administration and Management
The Construction Manager now has direct online access to all as-built drawings of the existing facilities, services, and utilities. This should expedite construction work generally, and it will also reduce any unplanned interruptions of services and utilities.

As always, you are welcome to attend our semi-monthly project review meeting. It will be held in the Main Boardroom of the existing ATB on Thursday, Nov 15th at 1:00 p.m.

Sincerely,

Jean-Francois Gourgon
Project General Manager

Project : (time estimate)

(print Project Time Estimate Letter on corporate letterhead paper)

January14, 20xx

Mr. Peter Chandler, Ph.D.
President and CEO
MicroTech Technologies Inc.
83 Ashbury Place
Montreal, QC H9R 3N5

Dear Mr. Chandler:

It was nice meeting with you and Michael Lee last Friday. Further to our discussion, attached is what I propose as the structure/outline for the MicroTech Business Plan, 20xx-20xx.

Below is my estimate of the level of effort that will be involved in producing a final Business Plan based on the attached outline and using the information in the documents that you provided me with:

Task Description	Time Estimate (hours)	Deliverable	Invoice on Delivery
Review and study all background material, develop outline of business plan, and conduct initial discussions with client.	10 to 15		
Develop first Draft of business plan for client review.	40 to 50	**Draft** Business Plan	Invoice No. 1
Discuss revisions with client, make revisions, and produce Draft Final business plan for final client review.	10 to 15	**Draft Final** Business Plan	
Produce Final version of business plan as per final client comments.	5 to 10	**Final** Business Plan	Invoice No. 2
Estimated Total	**65 to 90**		

This is my best estimate after carefully reviewing the documents you gave me. Of course, I would only bill for the actual professional time that I spend on the project. So, if it takes less time I will bill for less time. Since this is more than a standard writing job and has a business analysis component to it, the hourly rate I would normally charge would be $xx. However, since this is our first time doing business I am reducing this rate by 10% to $xx per hour.

The above estimate also assumes that I will produce a final electronic version of the plan for you (MS-Word), and that your company will look after all details and costs related to the production of a final hard copy report (I could look after this if required; it's just not included in the estimate).

If you require any additional information, please don't hesitate to contact me at (514) 998-1725.

Sincerely,

Roger R. Francis, M.B.A.

Attach. (1)

Project: (proposal acceptance)

(print Proposal Acceptance Letter on business letterhead paper)

October 12, 20xx

Ms. Mavis Treholme
Senior Partner
Barwick-Treholme Consulting Inc.
Briarwood Center, Suite 5-1700
1505 Riverview Drive
Lewisville, TX, 75025
972-217-3207

Dear Ms. Treholme:

Re: Community Attitudinal Survey – City Services

The purpose of this is to advise you that your firm, Barwick-Treholme Consulting Inc., has been selected as the successful bidder in response to our recent request for proposals for the "Conduct of an Attitudinal Survey Regarding the Provision of City Services". I congratulate you on your successful bid

The selection committee was impressed by the overall quality and depth of your proposal. As your lead contact for this project I look forward to working with you in ensuring that the survey is completed by the end of this calendar year and the draft report submitted to this office by January 31, 20xx.

I ask you to please call me as soon as possible so that we can set up a project initiation meeting. If you can't reach me through the main number, please feel free to call my mobile number at (972) 218-3245.

Yours sincerely,

Frank Schuller
City Manager

cc: Barbara Watters
    Director, Contracts Administration

Project: (proposal cover letter)

(print Proposal Cover Letter on corporate letterhead paper)

October 28, 20xx

Mr. Richard Tadeska
General Manager
Allied Manufacturing Inc.
15500 Marine View Drive
Seattle, WA 98165

Dear Mr. Tadeska:

On behalf of my partners at West Coast Construction Inc., I am pleased to submit the enclosed proposal for the design and construction of a new 30,000 square foot manufacturing facility at Allied's Westchester Park site.

We are well aware of Allied's leadership position in its sector and we fully understand your need for an advanced "state-of-the-art" manufacturing facility that will propel you to the next level in manufacturing and warehouse management and logistics. We believe that our firm is well-qualified to take you there. Your review of our proposal will no doubt confirm that.

As our proposal outlines, our company has designed and developed manufacturing and processing plants for customers in three different industrial sectors over the past few years. Two of these major projects are still in the final completion phase. Clearly, we do have the people and the know-how to take on a project like yours and give you a facility that will be admired throughout your industry.

We sincerely thank you for the opportunity to bid on this exciting project. We look forward to meeting with you soon to discuss our proposal in detail. Based on our understanding of your requirements, we are convinced that West Coast Construction would be the ideal partner for you in this major undertaking.

Sincerely,

Jackson Alexander
Senior Vice-President

Encl. (proposals – 5 copies)

Project: (proposal process)

(print Project Proposal Process Letter on corporate letterhead paper)

October 28, 20xx

Mr. Michael Haslem
Senior Partner
Adventis Consulting Inc.
3500 City View Road
Philadelphia, PA 19130

Dear Mr. Haslem:

Re: Customer Satisfaction Attitudinal Survey – Proposal Review Process – Phase 2

This is to advise you that the Proposal Review Committee (PRC) has accepted your Phase 1 proposal for the conduct of an attitudinal survey of users of city facilities and services. As a result, your firm has been placed on a short list of three companies which are being asked to participate in Phase 2 of the proposal selection process.

Phase 2 will involve an oral presentation allowing consultants to summarize, elaborate, and answer questions on the contents of their Phase I proposal. The general ground rules for Phase 2 are as follows:

- The oral presentation will be made to the PRC and will involve two (2) parts as follows: a 30 minute oral presentation, followed by a 30 minute question and answer session.

- Only those consultants included in the Phase 1 proposal will be eligible to attend the oral presentation.

- The oral presentations will take place on Tuesday November 25th in Boardroom B of the General Services Building, situated on Cityview Drive. To book a time, please call Marie Gervais of my office at (613) 728-4953.

- The score awarded by the PRC to the oral presentation will make up 35% of the total final score awarded to the consultant's overall proposal.

On behalf of the PRC, I thank you for your excellent written proposal and I look forward to your oral presentation on November 25th.

Sincerely,

Paul Matoyan
City General Manager

Project : (proposal submission)

(print Proposal Submission Letter on corporate letterhead paper)

June 27, 20xx

Rene Renata
CECOM Communications
2075 Victoria Avenue
Montreal, QC
J4S 1H1

Dear Rene:

Re: Twice Annual Newsletter For Home Safe Security Systems

Further to our recent phone discussion on the above-noted, and after reviewing the sample newsletter that you sent to me, my estimate and associated terms and assumptions follow:

- My charge to do the newsletter copywriting per 8-page issue would fall in the range of somewhere between $900 and $1,200. In addition, there would be a one-time charge of $250 to develop title concepts for review by the client and for participation in any required discussions while a choice is being made. This cost estimate is based on the following assumptions (as per our discussion):

- Writing of copy for an 8 page, 8 ½" x 11" English language newsletter containing approximately 2,000 words (+ or – 10%), as per sample dentist's newsletter that was supplied by CECOM (i.e. 8 pgs., approx. 2,100 words).

- This estimate covers straight copywriting, based on story ideas and material supplied by you and/or the primary client.

- The total number of articles focusing on different subjects will be in the range of four (4) to six(6).

- All layout, graphics, and printing-related work to be looked after by CECOM Communications and/or the primary client.

- Final Draft! will not be required to conduct original research to develop content for the newsletter. All background and research material will be supplied by CECOM and/or the primary client.

I trust that this is clear and gives you the information you need. Please call me at (514) 989-1765 if you have any questions.

Sincerely,

Robert Christian

OTHER BUSINESS-TO-BUSINESS LETTERS

These are miscellaneous business-to-business letters that don't fall clearly into one of the previous major business-to-business categories.

The following pages contain real-life templates of various uncategorized business-to-business letters.

Other Business-to-Business Letters

Note On Template Size

Please note that the letter templates on the following pages have been reduced in size slightly from what I consider ideal so that they could fit onto single pages of this guide. Because of this, the top and bottom margins are wider than what is recommended for a standard business letter (see pg 45). In addition, a point size of 11 has been used rather than the ideal size of 12 points.

Apology Letter: (serious error)

(print Apology Letter on corporate letterhead paper)

November 7, 20xx

Professor Bjorn Bergen
Professor of Aviation Management
Bishops College School of Business
750 King Edward Avenue
Toronto, ON, M5N 2E7

Dear Professor Bergen:

The purpose of this letter is to express my sincere apologies, on behalf of the International School of Aviation Management, for the errors and omissions that appeared in your listing and write-up in our Calendar of Courses for 20xx.

I heard that that you were quite offended by the mistakes when you received your copy of the Calendar recently. After reviewing the problems, I must say that I can quite understand your reaction, particularly when I see the number and extent of the errors in your listing.

The only explanation that I can offer is that an honest mistake was made by some of our staff in preparing the Calendar for printing. Somehow, in the rush to get everything into printing production at the last minute, your particular update sheet was overlooked. It was doubly unfortunate, since it appears that yours was the only case in which this happened.

As you know, the Calendars have all been mailed out internationally, so it is too late to stop and correct them. Nevertheless, I have met with the Director of Administration and we have come up with the following damage reduction plan.

- We will immediately print an erratum sheet and send it to all recipients of the Calendar.

- We will ensure that all corrections are made to the Website Course Calendar immediately, and a special note will be posted drawing attention to the revisions.

- We will ensure that all existing materials for courses that you will be teaching will be corrected, and that all new materials will reflect the correct information.

I trust that you will find these actions acceptable. If not, or if you have any other suggestions, please let us know at your earliest convenience.

Again, on behalf of the School of Business, my colleagues, and the staff, I sincerely apologize for this oversight, and hope that you will be understanding enough to accept our offer.

Very sincerely,

Johnson Bradley
Executive Director

c.c.: Elizabeth Johannsen, Director of Administration

Business Proposal: (set-up branch office)

(print Business Proposal letter on corporate or personal letterhead paper)

September 27, 20xx

Richard Cardiff
President - Daytime Solutions Inc.
2595 Meridian Drive, Suite 1400
St. Louis, MO 63105-3772

Dear Rick:

Please regard this letter as an expression of interest to establish a second DSI sales office in Toronto that will supplement and support the existing St.Louis office.

As you know, sustainability and longevity are important considerations for supporting any market. It is my belief that the current DSI network in Canada cannot, by itself, effectively handle the sales and support of DSI products in that market. My main reasons for making this proposal are summarized as follows:

- The current DSI network in Canada does not have the capability to support the current or future business requirements, without reliance on the St. Louis office. As you know, without a responsive support network that provides the high level of service that customers expect, use of DSI products will degrade quickly. This will leads to discontinued use of the products and negative testimonials about DSI.

- During the past five years I have established strong relationships of confidence and trust with all DSI customers with whom I have worked. I would like to continue building on that solid foundation by establishing my own sales and support network in Toronto. I believe strongly in the innovation and quality that of DSI products, and I would like to support those products with highly responsive support.

- I possess unique hands-on experience as an in-depth user of the DSI products. This expertise, combined with my skills and certification in Inventory Management, plus my extensive experience in sales, implementation and support; resulted in my customer accounts becoming the most referenced in DSI.

- Over the years I have refined a sales and follow-up approach that delivers results more quickly than most other DSI sales initiatives. By analyzing sales cycles and pursuing relationships with customers, I have developed unique lead-to-close strategies that fast-track results as never before achieved by DSI.

- I am personally responsible for a number of DSI successes of which you are aware. For example, I was instrumental in acquiring the Books World account in England. I was injected into the sales cycles targeting Worignal and Bests Inc. at the last minute and was still able to quickly convince those prospects that DSI is their best business choice. Before I left DSI, I made major sales presentations to Innovate, Sponagra, Mitectel and Reebro, all of which resulted in long-term contracts for DSI.

- I am convinced that the Canadian market has significant growth potential that can be exploited more thoroughly by establishing a second sales channel in Toronto. Indeed, I have no doubts that opening a second office here will result in at least double bottom-line growth within Canada.

I would really appreciate the opportunity to personally discuss with you the possibility of opening a Toronto operation. I therefore request that you contact me at your earliest convenience at (416) 274-5327.

I thank you in advance for your kind consideration and I hope to be speaking with you soon.

Very sincerely,

Frank Brandon

Commendation Letter: (customer service)

(Commendation from a private citizen normally printed on standard stationery)

September 20, 20xx

Ms. Vivien Lee
Manager, Guest Services
Royal Mount Hotel
2705 Sherbrooke Street W.
Montreal, H5S 3T7

Dear Ms. Lee:

Re: Exceptional Customer Service – Mr. Ernesto Suarez

My name is Ted Kaminski and I am Director of Corporate Services at Bushnell Biotech. Our company has had a corporate membership at your hotel's health and fitness club for over five years. I am writing this to you in your capacity as manager responsible for the club.

The sole purpose of this letter is to draw your attention to the exceptional level of service that has been provided by Mr. Ernesto Suarez since he joined the staff of the health club, some 18 months ago. I normally wouldn't take the time to write a letter like this, but in Ernesto's case, I just had to because he has made such a difference to the level of service that members now receive.

From the day he joined the team at the club it was clear that Ernesto was different from those who had preceded him. It was obvious from the beginning that he has a clear understanding of what customer service is all about, and he knows how to deliver it to club members.

Among many other things, Ernesto is extremely courteous, thoughtful, and kind in all of his dealings with members. In addition, he is very effective at running club matters. For example, previously, when a machine would break down (i.e. a treadmill) it would take anywhere from one to two weeks for it to be repaired due to lack of follow-up by health club staff. Now, when a machine breaks down, Ernesto makes it his personal mission to see that things are followed-up. Since he arrived, repairs are always done within 24 to 48 hours.

Before Ernesto, it was a common occurrence for the water coolers to be left unfilled, and the tissue boxes that should be kept outside of the squash courts would never be replaced without members complaining. Now with Ernesto in charge, these small but annoying things just don't happen anymore. He has instituted a "walk around" system whereby members of the health club staff must check all facilities at the beginning of their shift to see if anything needs attention. This has made a big difference and has definitely been noticed by members.

I have discussed my intention to write this letter with a number of regular members and they enthusiastically supported the idea that Ernesto be acknowledged for his exceptional efforts.

We trust that Ernesto Suarez will somehow be recognized for delivering a superior level of customer service to members of the Royal Mount Hotel Health and Fitness Club.

If you would like further details, please don't hesitate to contact me at (514) 972-4352.

Sincerely,

Ted Kaminski

Complaint Letter: (unacceptable service level)

(print Complaint Letter on personal or business letterhead, as appropriate)

November 12, 20xx

Richard Anderson
General Manager
BusNetwork Hosting Services
4500 Riverside Dr., Suite 225
Ottawa, ON, K2P 2C4

Dear Richard Anderson:

Re: Case No. 47716376 – SRS Website Unavailable For MoreThan 48 Hours

This is a follow-up to numerous telephone conversations I had with your customer service people between Oct. 6/06 and Oct. 9/06 regarding the unavailability of access to the SRS corporate Website space on BusNetwork servers for a period of more than two days.

We first noticed that access to our home page was not available around 10:00 p.m. on Wed. Oct. 6/06. At the time we assumed it was probably just a typical temporary condition that would be rectified in a matter of minutes; hours at worst. However, when I checked with staff here the next morning I was advised that the problem still existed. I called your customer service people late that morning and the people I spoke to there weren't even aware that the server on which the SRS Website resides had already been down for at least 12 hours! After checking out the situation your people advised me that technicians were working on the problem and it would be fixed as soon as possible. That was noon, Thursday October 7th.

From that point on; through the remainder of Thursday, and then throughout Friday, we continued to monitor the situation but were still not able to gain access to our Website. Finally, sometime around noon on Saturday October 9th I was advised by our staff that we were once again able to access our Website. So, according to my calculations those servers were inaccessible to SRS users for more than 48 hours.

In my experience, this kind of downtime for any type of business Web hosting service in this day and age is totally unacceptable. This company operates a total of twelve (12) Websites (some hosted elsewhere) and it is considered to be a serious problem by SRS staff if a server goes down for more than an hour. However, a server being unavailable for more than 48 hours is almost incomprehensible in modern business hosting. In fact, this is the poorest level of Web hosting service of which I have ever heard.

Whatever happened to capabilities such as mirror redundancy of data, and back-up servers that you could switch over to? Quite frankly, if I were a manager or technical professional at your company I would be truly embarrassed by this incident; especially for an established company such as yours.

SRS was one of BusNetwork's very first customers back in 1996 and we have stuck with you through thick and thin; and believe me there have indeed been some trying times over the years. However, we are now in the year 20xx and you have failed to properly provide basic hosting services that can be trusted.

We pay your company almost $350 per month for Web hosting and ancillary services. At this point I would like to know two things in particular: how/why this server access problem was allowed to go on for so long before it was corrected; and, have you taken measures to prevent such significant outages from occurring again? I look forward to receiving your reassurances in the near future.

In the spirit of excellent customer service,

Greig Palister

Congratulations Letter: (award winner)

(print Letter of Congratulations on corporate letterhead paper)

July 30, 20xx

Ms. Pamela Jacobsen
Director , Corporate Communications
AirVentures International Inc.
2450 Airport Drive
Pittsburgh, PA, 34295

Dear Pamela:

I just got back from spending time with you and our other IPRS colleagues at the annual conference and immediately heard the good news about your latest achievement from one of my colleagues here at Western Air Travel. Please accept my heartiest congratulations!

You must be so proud. After all, winning the "Bronson-Thompson Award for International Achievement in the Profession" is no easy feat. But, knowing how hard you worked on the Atlantis Multi-Media Project over the past three years, and seeing the awesome results that you achieved, I believe that you are a worthy recipient of this coveted distinction.

I spoke to Fred Perkins in Dallas yesterday and he was ecstatic to hear the news. Rick Trent and Marilyn Portman of this office also asked me to pass on their congratulations.

We were commenting at lunch yesterday that if you keep piling up the industry awards as you have been doing lately, you are going to have to build a trophy room soon. Also, Frank Cameron had better start watching his back, as you are clearly on a fast-track for his position!

I hope we will be able to get together for lunch next time you are in town. I would really like to pick your brain some more about the communications strategy you used on the Atlantis Project.

Again, please accept my sincere congratulations. I wish you many more such honors.

Sincere regards,

Fred W. Tucker
Director of Communications,

Invitation Letter: (conference speaker)

(print Letter of Invitation on corporate letterhead)

August 15, 20xx

Mr. Richard Berenson
Executive Director
Children With Disabilities Foundation
430 Smithson Drive, Suite 500
Chicago, IL 32956

Dear Mr. Berenson:

The purpose of this letter is to formally invite you, on behalf of the Board of Directors, to be the Closing Keynote Speaker at the upcoming 20xx IDCRI Conference.

The theme of this conference is "Disabling the Disability – Looking It Straight In the Eye". It will be held at the Mountainview Conference Facility, in Montpelier, Vermont from February 3 to 5, 20xx.

For you information, Susan Cruikshank of Taming the Environment will be the opening Keynote Speaker. The provisional title of her presentation is "The Disabled Environment – Can We Help It?". We will forward a complete draft speaker program to you in a couple of weeks to give you an idea of the specific subjects that will be covered by the other speakers.

We expect attendance this year to be the highest ever; in the area of 2,000 delegates and 150 speakers. This includes a large contingent from our new European Chapter that is based in Geneva. You may have hearsd that Dr. Gunther Berends will be presenting a major paper on his latest research into "Genetic Re-engineering". We are already receiving inquiries from all over the world about Dr. Berend's presentation.

In closing, we would be pleased and honored if you would consent to be our closing speaker at the 20xx ICDRI Conference.

I will call you in a week or so to follow up on this.

Yours sincerely,

Samuel Bagnall
Executive Director
International Disabled Children Research Institute

Justification: (laptop computer required)

(print Employee Commendation Memo on corporate letterhead paper)

MEMORANDUM

Date: September 20, 20xx

From: Marina Frampton

To: Juan Martinez - Director, Planning and Programs

Subject: <u>Request and Justification – Laptop Computer</u>

This is further to our recent discussion during which you asked for more information as to why I am requesting a laptop computer.

The primary reason why I need a laptop is that many of my duties require me to have frequent access to e-mail, Internet Websites, and the Alcoa network – all outside of normal working hours. A laptop computer would give me such access 24/7. Here are some specific examples that illustrate my need for a laptop.

Travel and Office Admin Support
- With William traveling so frequently, I often have to go into the office during off-hours to send urgent e-mails on his behalf when his Blackberry isn't working or he doesn't have computer/Internet access.

- When William calls me at home for support/assistance during off-hours, I can't properly support him because I don't have direct access to calendars and other documents on my hard drive at the office.

- There have also been times when Lloyd's flights have been delayed and I have had to go in to the office to reschedule his appointments at the last minute.

Global Team Support (Metrics and EHS)
- I often receive urgent Metric-related e-mail questions from Alcoans in various time zones around the world. Frequently, I am not able to respond to these queries on time because I can only access the system when I'm in the office during NY business hours.

- Bob conducts two Health topic Webinars per month. Since these start at 7:00 am local time, I have to be at the office at 6:30 am to set-up each session. With remote laptop access I could set these up from home.

- Similarily, I have to come in early for Pat's monthly Environmental Review Webinars. I also have to stay late to set-up Pat's Earthwatch sessions that Pat runs at 6:30 p.m. to accommodate staff working abroad.

- I also regularly monitor the EHS Helpdesk inbox and the AlcoaTrinidad inbox on an ongoing basis.

- I often receive urgent e-mails on Saturdays and Sundays from Earthwatch fellows during the selection process regarding; visa problems, rendezvous points, credit cards, first aid, and medical testing.

In addition to the above, access to the office network from home via laptop will allow me to provide support to EHS Awards, Earthwatch and Metrics, even when I am occasionally too sick to come to the office.

As you can see from the above, with a laptop providing me with from-home-access to the office network I will be a much more productive employee.

Thanks in advance for giving this your serious consideration.

Marina

Recognition Letter: (professional advice)

(print Recognition Letter on corporate letterhead stationery)

June 14, 20xx

Dr. Milton Grabchek, Ph.D.
Associate Professor
Department of Informatics
Independence University
1500 America Bouleverd
Raleigh, NC 27601

Dear Professor Grabchek:

On behalf of Lantos Search Technologies Inc., I would like to recognize you for the valuable assistance you have provided to our research and development department over the past two years. I am advised by Janet Gonzalez that your sage advice has been invaluable to the development of our latest search technology.

In particular, we very much appreciate that you gave freely of your time to assemble and organize the recent panel that we sponsored at the Innovations 20xx Conference on "Demystifying the Major Search Engines." You may be interested to know that the overall post-conference survey results reflected very favorably on that particular panel discussion. At LSTI we clearly recognize that your personal and professional contributions were pivotal to the success of that panel. I am told that its conclusions will figure prominently into the summary of proceedings which will be published next month.

For your information, I have attached a few of the post-conference comments we received about your panel from the survey of conference participants.

We trust that you enjoyed your time at the conference and we certainly look forward to your participation in next year's event.

Sincerely,

Bradley Pounder
President and CEO
Lantos Search Technologies Inc.

Reference Letter: (former customer)

(print Corporate Reference Letter on corporate letterhead paper)

November 20, 20xx

To Whom It May Concern:

Re: Customer Reference – Van Dusen Graphics Inc.

I have been asked to write this letter of reference because our company will no longer be operating its printing plant that has served Van Dusen Graphics Inc. for more than a decade.

Van Dusen Graphics has been one of our top customers for the past 12 years. Accordingly, I have no hesitation in recommending them as a company with which to do business.

In addition to doing business with his company for many years, Ray Van Dusen and I go back to our university days over 25 years ago. So, I can also personally vouch for him as a great individual and a concerned and active citizen in this community.

As far as a company to do business with, Van Dusen Graphics is one of the best that we have ever dealt with. Its practice was always to pay our printing invoices within the 30-day time limit. Our two companies did significant amounts of business, especially during the past 5 years, and I cannot recall a late-payment situation. Billing disputes were rare, and those only required some minor additional documentation for clarification and resolution.

Van Dusen was one of the best companies that I have ever dealt with from a change-order and work scheduling perspective. We maintained a close communication with the company's production people and they always kept us apprised of their upcoming workload, so that scheduling jobs on our presses was never a problem. In addition, Van Dusen's graphics people always provided us with high quality finished artwork, and it was unusual for additional changes to be made after the plates had been produced.

Based on our experience, any printing company should be very pleased to be the one that Van Dusen Graphics chooses to do business with once we have closed our doors.

Sincerely,

Edward Wallendar
President and CEO

Thank You: (professional assistance)

(print corporate Thank You Letter on corporate letterhead paper)

November 30, 20xx

Mr. David Kimberly
Director General, Civil Aviation
Government of Seychelles
10 Island View Parkway
Seychelles

Dear David,

I would like to take this opportunity to express my heartfelt thanks to you for your very active participation in our recent conference in Montreal on the "future of aviation". The Chairman and Board Members have also asked me to pass on their sincere appreciation for your efforts in supporting the Institute in this important undertaking.

Your skill in chairing the controversial panel on "The Role of Developing Countries in the Future of Aviation Management" was very much appreciated by those representing all sides of that extremely sensitive topic. As well, we have received numerous post-conference requests for the paper you delivered on "The Critical Issue of Cooperation Between Airlines and Airports." It appears that you may have penned a best-seller with that one!

On both a professional and a personal level, I really appreciated the time that the two of us were able to spend together for fun and reflection during conference down times. I certainly learned a lot about the unique aspects of aviation operations in your part of the world (not to mention the things you taught me about the backhand on the squash court!).

We are currently hard at work producing the "Compendium of Conference Proceedings" document, and we expect to be sending it out to all participants early in the new year.

Again, thanks so much for your enthusiastic participation in our conference. I have no doubt that it would not have been the success that it was without your presence.

Please keep in touch, and drop in and visit us whenever you are in this part of the world.

Very sincerely,

Peter Smithfield
President and CEO

Thank You: (fund-raising assistance)

(print Business Thank You Letter on corporate letterhead paper)

March 15, 20xx

Mr. Alphonse Germanian
President and CEO
BioDynamics Llc.
1525 Broadway, Suite 4500
New York, NY 10034

Dear Mr. Germanian:

As Chairperson of the Corporate Conscience Campaign - *Helping the Homeless in New York*, I am writing this to thank you personally for your company's support in last month's fund-raising effort.

As I indicated when we spoke on the phone two weeks ago, the campaign was considered a resounding success, raising a total of $1.65 million to-date, significantly exceeding our target of $1 million. Some donations are still trickling in, so we could end up close to a total of $2 million!

BioDynamics was an influential leader throughout the entire three-month campaign. In fact, we couldn't have succeeded without the generous support of your company, both financially, and through your organizational and administrative assistance. Your Team Leader, Kathryn Gomez was particularly impressive, going above and beyond what we could have expected of someone performing as a volunteer while continuing on with her day-to-day duties. Please convey my special thanks to Kathryn.

I would also ask you to convey my sincere thanks and congratulations to all of those other people in your company who contributed in any way to the Helping the Homeless Campaign. Please tell them that the sum of their contributions resulted in a major success that they should all be proud of taking part in.

I believe that the 27 companies that participated in this effort have set a new standard for social responsibility in this community, and have set a powerful example that will inspire other companies and organizations to do the same.

I look forward to seeing you at the Mayor's special thank you reception next month.

Yours sincerely,

Jackson Pritchard
Fundraising Chair

BUSINESS-TO-CUSTOMER LETTERS

This section of the manual contains 44 fully-formatted real-life templates for the most common types of letters used in day-to-day business correspondence when dealing with customers in the form of every day consumers.

For easy reference, here are the categories and the sample letters included in each:

Covering Letters (pg. 143)

Company Information
Franchise Application
Product Shipment

Customer Relations Letters (pg. 147)

Complaint Response
Follow-Up – New Customer
Interrupted Service Notice
Letter Acknowledgement
Price Increase Notice
Special Invitation
Thanks For Suggestion
Welcome New Customer

Financial and Credit Letters (pg. 157)

Collection Letter, Initial Notice
Collection Letter, Second Notice
Collection Letter, Third Notice
Collection Letter, Final Notice
Collection Letter, Delinquency Notice
Credit Approval
Credit Denial
Invoice, Professional Services

Introduction Letters (pg. 167)

New Loans Manager
New Service Available
New Service Representative

Order-Related Letters (pg. 171)

Backorder Notice
Delayed Order Notice
Order Acknowledgement
Order Confirmation
Order Fulfillment
Partial Order Notice
Product Unavailable

Sales and Marketing Letters (pg. 179)

Exclusive Member Mailing
Personalized Sales Letter
Product Sales Mailer
Leave-Behind Letter
Solicit Former Customer
Targeted Customer Mailer

Other Business-to-Customer Letters (pg. 187)

Announcement – New Location
Apology – Customer Service Error
Condolence – Long-Time Customer
Congratulations – Former Employee
Follow-Up – After Conference Contact
Follow-Up – After In-Store Contact
Fundraising – Community Project
Reference – Former Customer
Thank You - Customer Survey Participation

For more business-to-customer letters see the Third Edition letters on page 197.

Note On Template Size

Please note that the letter templates on the following pages have been reduced in size slightly from what I consider ideal so that they could fit onto single pages of this guide. Because of this, the top and bottom margins are wider than what is recommended for a standard business letter (see pg. 45). In addition, a point size of 11 has been used rather than the ideal size of 12 points.

COVERING LETTERS

A business-to-customer "covering letter" is one that a company typically uses to transmit documents such as corporate brochures, marketing and promotional material, and products to their customers. Normally, the customer will have requested the particular document first. These are sometimes referred to as "transmittal letters" or "letters of transmittal".

The following pages contain some real-life templates of business-to-customer covering letters.

Covering Letters

Note On Template Size

Please note that the letter templates on the following pages have been reduced in size slightly from what I consider ideal so that they could fit onto single pages of this guide. Because of this, the top and bottom margins are wider than what is recommended for a standard business letter (see pg 45). In addition, a point size of 11 has been used rather than the ideal size of 12 points.

Cover: (company information)

(print Cover Letter on business letterhead paper)

August 30, 20xx

Mr Harvey Richardson
2672 Carling Ave.
Suite 1502
Ottawa, ON
K1A 0N8

Dear Mr. Richardson:

Further to your e-mail request of August 28, enclosed is a copy of Hartford's Annual Report for the financial year 20xx-20xx.

To give you a bit more background on the company, I have also taken the liberty of enclosing a corporate brochure and a prospectus for our upcoming Initial Public Offering (IPO). As you may be aware from reading the business press, that IPO is set to take place next month.

If you have any additional questions about the company after reviewing the enclosed information, please feel free to give me a call at 235-9879. If I'm not able to answer your questions I will be able to put you in touch with someone who will.

Thanks very much for your interest in Hartford Industries.

Yours sincerely,

Theresa Remington
Communications Officer

Enclosures (3)

Cover: (franchise application)

(print Cover Letter on business letterhead paper)

February 25, 20xx

Mrs Florence Henderson
32 Kirby Avenue
Somerbville NJ
08876

Dear Mrs. Henderson:

Further to your recent telephone request, enclosed is a blank Franchise Application with a set of instructions for its completion. I have also enclosed a Craft City corporate brochure and a franchise fees schedule.

If after reviewing these documents you decide that you would like to proceed with acquiring a Craft City business franchise, please contact me and I will arrange for an immediate meeting with our business development team. The people in that group will be able to answer any technical or financial questions that you may have.

I can be reached during office hours at 210-345-2789, and after hours at 210-232-4973.

I look forward to hearing from you.

Yours sincerely,

Francesca Clayton
Senior Business Associate

Enclosures (3)

Cover: (product shipment)

(print Cover Letter on business letterhead paper)

December 10, 20xx

Mr Julio Chavez
1825 Marymount Ave.
Marina Del Ray, CA
90294

Dear Mr. Chavez:

Congratulations on becoming the owner of a new Quantum Computer System!

The purpose of this letter is to confirm to you what should be included in the shipment that you have just received and to tell you how to get in touch with us. The shipment should have comprised three (3) boxes as follows:

1.   Dimension 4500 personal computer in a tower case.

2.   19" color monitor with flat screen definition.

3.   One pair of Harmon Kardon speakers.

Each box includes a detailed packing slip itemizing the specific contents and technical specifications. Box number 1 also includes the quick start instructions to follow when setting up your computer.

If you have any questions at all about your new system you can sign on to our Website at www.quantumcomputer.com (if you have Internet access), or you can call our customer service center toll free at 1-800-605-7500 (8:00 a.m. to 11:00 p.m. EST).

We thank you for purchasing a Quantum Computer and we trust that you will enjoy your new system.

Yours sincerely,

Michael Hunter
Vice-President, Customer Satisfaction

Enclosures (3)

CUSTOMER RELATIONS LETTERS

A business-to-customer "customer relations letter" is one that a company typically sends to customers on an individual basis that deals with specific issues related to the relationship between the company and that customer.

Typical "customer relations letters" include thank you letters and responses to inquiries and complaints.

The following pages contain real-life templates of business-to-customer "customer relations letters".

Customer Relations Letters

Note On Template Size

Please note that the letter templates on the following pages have been reduced in size slightly from what I consider ideal so that they could fit onto single pages of this guide. Because of this, the top and bottom margins are wider than what is recommended for a standard business letter (see pg 45). In addition, a point size of 11 has been used rather than the ideal size of 12 points.

Customer Relations: (complaint response)

(print Customer Relations Letter on business letterhead paper)

November 23, 20xx

Mr. Pablo Perrera
1820 Whitfield Park Road
Apartment 1510
Sarasota, FL 34242

Dear Mr. Perrera:

I am writing this to offer my sincere apologies on behalf of the Guests First Hotel Corporation. Specifically, I am referring to your recent letter of complaint about the inadequate health club facilities and services that you experienced at our Cleveland location when you registered for the "Weekend Health Club Special" on Friday October 25th.

Unfortunately, the weekend you stayed at our Cleveland hotel there were a number of serious problems at the Health Club. I understand that the swimming pool was closed on Saturday, the whirlpool was out of service for the entire weekend, two jogging machines were broken, and there was no daycare available as promised.

You are absolutely right to be upset of course. In our business this is an unacceptable level of service. Frankly, as a long time professional in the hospitality business, I must say that I was embarrassed when I checked into your complaint and realized the extent of the problems you faced that weekend. I can't offer any reasonable explanation except to say that we failed. What I can say is that it won't happen again if I have anything to do with it.

To reassure you that we are taking your complaint very seriously, I want you to know that a directive has been issued to our entire network of hotels advising them of your experience and how it is totally unacceptable. In addition, a number of serious measures have been taken at our Cleveland hotel to make sure there is never a repeat of such a situation.

I realize that we can't fully compensate you for the inconvenience and frustration that you experienced in one of our hotels. However, we would like to offer you some compensation as a way of asking you to give Guests First another chance.

Accordingly, enclosed is a check for $199 in full refund for your accommodation on the weekend of October 25th. In addition, I have enclosed a letter addressed to any Hotel General Manager in our North American network entitling you and one guest to two nights of free accommodation (double occupancy) at whichever hotel you choose. To use it, simply make a reservation in advance giving the authorization number at the top of that letter (instead of credit card number) and then present the original of the letter at the registration desk when you check in.

Yours sincerely,

Beverly Whitcombe
Vice-President, Guest Services

Enclosures (2)

Customer Relations: (follow-up new customer)

(print Customer Relations Letter on business letterhead paper)

October 5, 20xx

Mr. David Halldon
795 Center Ave.
Ann Arbor, MI 48102

Dear Mr. Halldon:

I was very pleased to meet you last Thursday at our Customer Appreciation Event. I hope you enjoyed seeing the new Suzuki models as much as we enjoyed showing them off!

As a two-time Suzuki owner, you no doubt appreciated the new, more sophisticated, package that Suzuki has come up with for all of its vehicles for the upcoming model year. As you remarked that evening, the company does indeed bundle so much into the basic package that there's hardly a need for options. I would tend to agree with that assessment – unless you're into driving a luxury high-tech package of course.

I would like to take this opportunity to invite you back to the dealership to take a test drive in the new AWD High Terrain SUV that you were sitting in at our event. I know that your current lease will be expiring in December, so may I suggest that you call me sometime during the next few weeks for a test drive appointment whenever it's convenient for you. You can reach me via cellular phone at 645-3790. If I'm not answering for some reason please leave a message and I'll get back to you as soon as I can.

It just so happens that your lease expiry date is perfect timing for you to get an excellent deal on whatever Suzuki model you might choose. Suzuki America just announced last week that they are offering lease financing at 0% interest until December 31, 20xx. Let's hope you can take advantage of that.

I look forward to hearing from you so that we can arrange to take you out for a test drive. I would be pleased to brief you on whichever Suzuki models you may be interested in for your next lease. Again, please call me at 645-3790 and I will be pleased to make the arrangements at your convenience.

Always at your service,

Susan Zemeckis
Senior Sales Associate

Customer Relations: (interrupted service notice)

(print Customer Relations Letter on business letterhead paper)

May 25, 20xx

Residents of Marina Vista
4500 Carling Ave.
Ottawa, ON
K2G 0P9

To All Residents:

Re: Repairs and Re-paving - Underground Parking Garage – June 12–16, 20xx

On behalf of Condominium Corporation 668125 I am sending this to all residents of Marina Vista to advise you of how the upcoming repairs to the parking garage will affect you during the 5-day period, June 12 to 16, inclusive.

During that period, the entire parking garage will be unavailable to residents. Following are the arrangements we have made to try to minimize the impact on residents while these much needed repairs are being carried out.

- All vehicles must be removed from the parking garage prior to 7:00 a.m. on June 12th. If you have a vehicle that does not run or that requires a tow for some other reason, please contact Bob at the Corporation office at 734-5945 and he will make the necessary arrangements.

- Vehicles that are normally parked on Level 1 of the garage can be parked in outside Lots 1 and 2 for the duration of the repairs. If you have a permit for Level 1 of the garage, we will issue you with a special windshield sticker prior to June 12th.

- All vehicles that are normally parked on Levels 2 and 3 of the garage can be parked directly across Carling Avenue on the Super Store parking lot for the duration of the repairs. Those with permits for Levels 2 and 3 will be given special windshield stickers prior to June 12th.

Please note that it is very important that you display your windshield sticker during this period so that the security patrol does not tow your car away by mistake.

We thank you in advance for your co-operation during this period and we apologize for any inconvenience that this may cause. If you have any questions or concerns please feel free to call Bob at the office at 734-5945, or me at 772-3456.

Sincerely,

Carl Underwood
President, C.C. 668125

Customer Relations: (letter acknowledgement)

(print Customer Relations Letter on business letterhead paper)

July 14, 20xx

Ms. Veronica Lancombe
145 Randolph Avenue
Apartment 2915
Chicago, IL 60605

Dear Ms. Lancombe:

Thank you for your letter of July 12 in which you requested more details about the publications that we offer.

Your letter has been forwarded to Heather Small our Production and Distribution Co-ordinator. She will assemble a package of publicity flyers and brochures, plus our latest catalogue, and mail them to you later this week. You should receive the package in about 10 days.

We appreciate your interest in Final Draft Publications and have added your name and address to our publicity mailing list.

Sincerely,

Robert James
Director, Marketing and Sales

Customer Relations: (price increase notice)

(print Customer Relations Letter on business letterhead paper)

November 1, 20xx

[Customer Mailing List]
[Customer Address line 2]
[Customer Address line 3]
[Customer Address line 4]

Dear [Name of Customer]:

Subject: Notice of Price Increase – Effective January 1, 20xx

I regret to inform you that due to circumstances beyond our control we will be forced to increase the prices of all of our products by 5% to 10%, as of January1, 20xx.

As you can well imagine, this was not an easy decision for this company. In fact, we have not had an across-the-board price increase in more than a decade. The new price list is enclosed.

Nevertheless, the situation finally reached a critical point this year where we felt we had no choice. The continuing devaluation of the US Dollar against most major currencies, the onslaught of bottom-dollar competitors from certain developing countries, and the relentless increases in pulp and paper prices, have given us no choice if we are to stay in business delivering quality paper products to our valued customers.

As CEO of Paper Products International, you have my personal commitment that this company will continue to provide you with the highest quality finished paper products on the planet. We may have been forced to increase our prices by external forces beyond our control, but nothing will ever force this company to compromise its industry leading reputation for producing the best products in the business.

We have announced this increase two months in advance in order to give you time to adjust your operations and planning as may be required. Please don't hesitate to contact your Marketing PPI Representative should you have any questions about this price increase and its impacts.

On behalf of the PPI Board and all of our staff I would like to thank you in advance for your understanding and cooperation on this matter. As always, our number one priority at PPI is to be "The first in quality".

Yours Sincerely,

Reg Schacter
President and CEO

Encl: PPI Price List – 20xx

Customer Relations: (special invitation)

(print Customer Relations Letter on business letterhead paper)

January 20, 20xx

Mrs. Bianca Benedict
1541 Notre-Dame West
Suite No. 7
Montreal, QC
H3C 1L2

Dear Mrs. Benedict:

Re: Private Preview Showing – Spring Collection 20xx – Ticket No. 798435-2

As one of our longtime valued customers we would like to invite you to our special Private Preview Showing of our Spring Fashion Collection for 20xx.

The showing will take place at our downtown store at 4550 Sherbrooke St. West, **Monday evening, February 20, 20xx** from 7:00 pm to 11:00 pm. Limited free parking will be available in our parking garage on the Mountain Street side of the store.

In addition to the continuous fashion show that will be running all evening long, there will be a number of spring merchandise draws, as well as a door prize for a $2,000 unlimited shopping spree. So, don't miss out on the fun!

For entry into the show and to be eligible for any of the draws you will be required to produce **this original invitation with your ticket number** printed on it.

In order that we may plan for snacks and refreshments appropriately, if you plan to attend, we ask you to please call Danielle Laporte at (514) 982-7593 and advise her by February 10th.

Please note: If Danielle doesn't hear from you by Friday, February 10th we will assume that you are not attending the show and we will issue your ticket number to someone else.

Everyone here at The Fashion House looks forward to meeting you and sharing our Spring Collection with you at our Preview Private Showing.

Yours sincerely,

Rhonda Sugarman
Show Co-ordinator

Customer Relations: (thanks for suggestion)

(print Customer Relations Letter on business letterhead paper)

January 20, 20xx

Mr. Walter Ambruzio
2150 Irving Street
Allenville, ME 03910

Dear Mr. Ambruzio:

I would like to thank you for your recent letter in which you made numerous suggestions for improvements to the services and facilities at the FitLife Health Club.

I won't address each of your suggestions here, they are so numerous, but I will say that many of them appear at first glance to be excellent. I particularly like what you had to say about some of the procedures related to entering and leaving the swimming pool and dressing room areas.

As it turns out, your timing for sending this letter was perfect. Our internal "Facilities and Services Review Committee" is scheduled to meet the week after next. This will give me time to circulate a copy of your letter to committee members in advance, so that we may put it on the agenda for discussion at that meeting.

I should be able to let you know what comes out of that process by mid-February. If you haven't heard from me by then, please give me a call at 735-2945, or drop in at my office at the Club and I will update you on the status of things.

On behalf of the FitLife Management Team, I sincerely thank you for the time and trouble you took in making these suggestions.

Yours sincerely,

Joffre McMaster
Health Club General Manager

Customer Relations: (welcome new customer)

(print Customer Relations Letter on business letterhead paper)

June 28, 20xx

Mr. and Mrs. Stuart Hartley
280 Heath Drive
Victoria, BC
V9A 2J5

Dear Mr. and Mrs. Hartley:

Welcome to Victoria Estates!

I was just advised by Karen, one of our front desk customer service agents, that you and your family have recently moved into our neighborhood. I would like to personally welcome you.

You've made an excellent choice on where to put down roots, if only for a while. I'm sure that you and your three children will love this closely knit little neighborhood we have here. Great people, good schools, lots of parkland, and a very active community association are what make this one of the most desirable communities to live in anywhere in the province.

In addition to welcoming you as a neighbor, as President of the local merchants association I would also like to welcome you on behalf of my fellow merchants. You'll find that Victoria Estates has an exceptional group of small merchants and service companies ready to serve you with competitive prices and a focus on customer service.

As President and Owner of Clean Rite Dry Cleaning Systems Inc., I would like to offer you a welcome wagon special for new members in our community, as follows. For three(3) months from the date of this letter your entire family is eligible for a 15% discount off of our regular prices for all dry cleaning work that is done by Clean Rite. In fact, I have taken the liberty of having the staff enter your family name and address into the computer so that the moment someone in your family drops something off for cleaning, the discount will be applied automatically.

We look forward to serving you and getting to know you.

Yours sincerely,

Ron Barron
President

FINANCIAL AND CREDIT LETTERS

Business-to-customer "financial and credit letters" can be both administrative and promotional in nature.

Typical examples include such correspondence as: invoices and account statements, as well as increases in credit limits, and approvals and non-approvals of credit limits.

The following pages contain real-life templates of business-to-customer financial and credit letters.

Financial and Credit Letters

Collection, Initial Notice (pg. 158)
Collection, Second Notice (pg. 159)
Collection, Third Notice (pg. 160)
Collection, Final Notice (pg. 161)
Collection, Delinquency Notice (pg. 162)
Credit Approval (pg.)
Credit Denial (pg. 164)
Invoice, Professional Services (pg. 165)

Note On Template Size

Please note that the letter templates on the following pages have been reduced in size slightly from what I consider ideal so that they could fit onto single pages of this guide. Because of this, the top and bottom margins are wider than what is recommended for a standard business letter (see pg 45). In addition, a point size of 11 has been used rather than the ideal size of 12 points.

Financial and Credit: (collection letter, initial)

(print Financial and Credit Letters on business letterhead paper)

June 18, 20xx

Mr. Dylan Macdonald
150 Armstrong Ave.
Georgetown, ON
L7G 5S4

Dear Mr. Macdonald:

Re: Invoice 279-02 - May 30, 20xx - $1,755.68

This is just a reminder that the above-noted invoice is now overdue. All of our invoices are due in full within 30 days of the invoice date.

Would you please remit **$1,755.68** today.

If you have already mailed your payment, please disregard this letter.

Thanks very much,

B. R. Egan
Accounts Receivable

BRE:st

Financial and Credit: (collection letter, second)

(print Financial and Credit Letters on business letterhead paper)

July 15, 20xx

Mr. Dylan Macdonald
150 Armstrong Ave.
Georgetown, ON
L7G 5S4

Dear Mr. Macdonald:

Second Notice: Re: Invoice 279-02 - May 30, 20xx - $1,755.68

Our records indicate that the above-noted balance remains unpaid. If there is some problem affecting this invoice that we may be unaware of, would you please give me a call at 725-9943.

Otherwise, we would ask you to please submit the full amount of **$1,755.68** today.

If you have already taken action to pay this, please ignore this notice.

Thank you,

B. R. Egan
Accounts Receivable

BRE:st

cc: M.S. Brandon, Credit Manager

Financial and Credit: (collection letter, third)

(print Financial and Credit Letters on business letterhead paper)

July 30, 20xx

Mr. Dylan Macdonald
150 Armstrong Ave.
Georgetown, ON
L7G 5S4

Hand Delivered By Courier

Dear Mr. Macdonald:

Third Notice: Re: Invoice 279-02 - May 30, 20xx - $1,755.68

According to our records, the above-noted invoice for the amount of **$1,755.68** is still unpaid.

We assume that there must have been some oversight at your end and we understand that these things happen from time to time. Nevertheless, we would ask you to please remit payment immediately.

If there is some problem preventing the payment of this invoice would you please contact our Credit Manager, Mr. M.S. Brandon and he would be happy to discuss the matter with you.

If you have already sent your payment, we thank you, and ask you to please disregard this letter.

Sincerely,

B. R. Egan
Accounts Receivable

BRE:st

cc: M.S. Brandon, Credit Manager

Financial and Credit: (collection letter, final appeal)

(print Financial and Credit Letters on business letterhead paper)

August 16, 20xx

Mr. Dylan Macdonald
150 Armstrong Ave.
Georgetown, ON
L7G 5S4

Hand Delivered By Courier

Dear Mr. Macdonald:

Final Notice: Re: Invoice 279-02 - May 30, 20xx - $1,755.68

You have repeatedly ignored our written requests for payment of the above-noted invoice and you have not contacted us with any explanation.

Consequently, unless we receive payment in full by the end of the business day, August 30, 20xx we will have to take the unpleasant step of turning your account over to a professional collection agency. We would rather not do this since it will result in damage to your personal credit rating.

To prevent us from taking the final step of turning this matter over to a collection agency, could you please make payment in full by the end of the business day, Friday August 30, 20xx.

We urge you to please give this matter your full attention now, before it's too late, and send your payment to us immediately.

Sincerely,

B. R. Egan
Accounts Receivable

BRE:st

cc: M.S. Brandon, Credit Manager

Financial and Credit: (collection letter, delinquency)

(print Financial and Credit Letters on business letterhead paper)

August 30, 20xx

Mr. Dylan Macdonald
150 Armstrong Ave.
Georgetown, ON
L7G 5S4

Hand Delivered By Courier

Dear Mr. Macdonald:

Delinquency Notice: Re: Invoice 279-02 - May 30, 20xx - $1,755.68

Our repeated appeals for payment of the above-noted invoice have been consistently ignored. We therefore regard your account as delinquent.

This is to advise you that effective Monday September 2, 20xx your account will be turned over to Action Plus Collections Corporation. We have instructed that agency to pursue the collection of this outstanding account with due haste.

If you wish to discuss the matter before that company commences its collection operation against you, please contact Mr. R. Hardinski of that company immediately. He can be reached at 745-2398.

Sincerely,

M.S. Brandon
Credit Manager

BRE:st

cc: B.R. Egan, Accounts Receivable
    R. Hardinski, Action Plus Collections

Financial and Credit: (credit approval)

(print Financial and Credit Letters on business letterhead paper)

November 15, 20xx

Ms. Marilyn Lithwack
401 Hollis Street
Emeryville, CA 94608

Dear Ms. Lithwack:

We are pleased to inform you that we have completed our review of your credit card application and you have been approved to receive a Thompson's Gold Card in your name.

Based on the information you gave us, we have set your initial credit limit at $3,000. After you have been with us for one year you may request a revision to that amount. Your card should arrive at your home address by registered mail next week. When you receive it, please make sure you follow the instructions in that letter in order to activate your card.

We thank you for requesting a Thompson's credit card and we look forward to a long and harmonious relationship with you as a valued cardholder.

Yours sincerely,

R.K. Brackston
Manager, Credit Services

RKB:lm

Financial and Credit: (credit denial)

(print Financial and Credit Letters on business letterhead paper)

November 15, 20xx

Mr. Vincent Cambridge
165 West Grand Road
Tucson, AZ 85745

Dear Mr. Cambridge:

We regret to inform you that we will be unable to offer you credit at this time. Our review of your application, coupled with your recent record indicated that you have had some difficulty in meeting your financial obligations over the past few years.

Once you have managed to rectify your financial uncertainties we would be pleased to review your application for credit again. Our policy states that a credit application must have a minimum of one full year of completely clean credit record time before we consider a credit application.

We thank you for your application and wish you all the best. We hope to be able to call you one of our valued credit card customers in the future.

Yours sincerely,

Vivien Franchitti
Credit Services

VSF:sr

Financial and Credit: (invoice, professional services)

(print Financial Letters on business letterhead paper)

INVOICE 02-047

To:	**David Kingsley** 374 Laurentian Ave. Montreal, QC H3C 1L2	**From:**	**Robert Williams** (as per above)

Fax	(516) 954-6376	Pages:	1

Phone:	(516) 954-8222	Date:	**Nov. 26, 20xx**
Re:	**Development of Resume, Cover Letter,** **and Bonus Career Brief**	CC:	

Please regard this as an INVOICE for English editorial services provided while developing your resume/cv and a cover letter. Package includes a Bonus 300 word Career Brief. Work was performed Nov. 20 to 25/02. Final copy submitted to Client by e-mail on Nov. 25/02.

English Editorial Services	5.0 hours at $ 60.00 per hr.	=	$	300.00
GST at 7.0% (142687426)				21.00
QST at 7.5% (101394564)				24.08

TOTAL Amount Owing (payable <u>within 30 days</u> of Invoice date)   = $ **345.08**

Thanks very much for this work. Please don't hesitate to contact me should you have a requirement for editorial or consulting services in the future.

Sincerely,

Robert Williams

INTRODUCTION LETTERS

A business-to-customer "introduction letter" or "letter of introduction" is one that a company uses to introduce itself, its products or services, or one of its representatives, to its customer list.

The following pages contain real-life templates of business-to-customer introduction letters.

Introduction Letters

Note On Template Size

Please note that the letter templates on the following pages have been reduced in size slightly from what I consider ideal so that they could fit onto single pages of this guide. Because of this, the top and bottom margins are wider than what is recommended for a standard business letter (see pg 45). In addition, a point size of 11 has been used rather than the ideal size of 12 points.

Introduction: (new loans manager)

(print Introduction Letters on business letterhead paper)

April 18, 20xx

Send To Client List
Client Address - Line 2
Client Address - Line 3
Client Address - Line 4
Client Address - Line 5

Dear [Client Name]:

The purpose of this is to advise you that we now have a new Personal Loans Manager here at Nation Wide Bank. Her name is Catherine Wong, and she joins us after completing a five year assignment at our Customer Service Center in Dallas.

I'm sure you will find Catherine to be a very pleasant professional to deal with. She is a very people-friendly type of person, and she has received specialized training in personalized customer service considerations and techniques. She also holds a Masters of Business Administration degree from
Dartmouth College.

Please feel free to say hello to Catherine the next time you are in at the branch doing your banking. Or if you like, you can give her a call at 823-5621 to discuss your personal financial needs.

I'm sure that you will join me in welcoming Catherine to our branch. I know that she looks forward to meeting each and every one of our valuable clients.

Yours sincerely,

Grant Cumberland
Branch General Manager

Introduction: (new service available)

(print Introduction Letters on business letterhead paper)

March 15, 20xx

Send To Customer List
Customer Address - Line 2
Customer Address - Line 3
Customer Address - Line 4
Customer Address - Line 5

Dear [Customer Name]:

New Child Care Center For Busy Parents

This is to let you know that on April 1, 20xx we will be introducing our brand new state-of-the-art Customer Child Care Center at our downtown location on University Street.

We have taken this initiative because we talked to our customers and you told us that such a service ranks high on your priority list. We listened to you. Then we hired one of the best experts available for designing such programs and facilities, Dr. Claire Reinholdt. As most of you will know, Dr. Reinholdt is a successful and highly respected child psychologist who has penned two best-selling books about her specialty.

We told Dr. Reinholdt that our general requirement was for a child care program and facility at which people could leave their children in a safe and educational environment for periods of between one and four hours while they shopped in our store. What she has designed is a leading-edge program and facility, staffed by accredited professionals, that is one-of-a kind in North America.

We invite you to take advantage of this new service the next time you are in the market for anything from clothing , to furniture, to home appliances.

Not only will you be well taken care of by our professional sales staff, your children will be in the safe care of the professionals at our new Customer Child Care Center.

We look forward to seeing your whole family!

Yours very sincerely,

Charlotte Renfrew
Vice-President, Customer Services

Introduction: (new service representative)

(print Introduction Letters on business letterhead paper)

January 30, 20xx

Send To Customer List
Customer Address - Line 2
Customer Address - Line 3
Customer Address - Line 4
Customer Address - Line 5

Dear [Customer Name]:

New Service Manager – David Callaghan - West End Suzuki Inc.

I am very pleased to be able to introduce to you our new Customer Service Manager, David Callaghan. David joined the West End customer service team January 15, 20xx.

David is truly an exceptional find in this industry.

He brings with him an impressive and well-rounded 17-year record in the automotive maintenance, sales, and service industry. He spent the first five years as a maintenance mechanic, followed by eight years in vehicle sales, and he has worked as a customer service representative for the past four years. You won't find many people who know the business from all of the major aspects like David does.

In his previous position as a customer service representative, David won one National Award and one Regional Commendation for excellence in customer service.

In his new position, David will be pleased to look after all of your vehicle maintenance needs. A real people person, he looks forward to getting to know all of our customers, both old and new.

I urge you to give David a call at 238-4593 and book your next regular maintenance appointment with him. Tell him about this letter and he will apply a 10% discount to your next servicing appointment.

I'm sure you'll join me in welcoming David personally the next time you bring your vehicle in to West End for servicing.

Yours sincerely,

Bob Crampton
President and Owner

ORDER-RELATED LETTERS

A business-to-customer "order-related letter" is one that a company normally uses to advise a customer as to the status of an order they have made for a product or service.

The following pages contain real-life templates of business-to-customer "order-related letters".

Order-Related Letters

Backorder Notice (pg. 172)
Delayed Order Notice (pg. 173)
Order Acknowledgement (pg. 174)
Order Confirmation (pg. 175)
Order Fulfillment (pg. 176)
Partial Order Notice (pg. 177)
Product Unavailable (pg. 178)

Note On Template Size

Please note that the letter templates on the following pages have been reduced in size slightly from what I consider ideal so that they could fit onto single pages of this guide. Because of this, the top and bottom margins are wider than what is recommended for a standard business letter (see pg 45). In addition, a point size of 11 has been used rather than the ideal size of 12 points.

Order-Related: (backorder notice)

(print Order-Related Letters on business letterhead paper)

June 14, 20xx

Mr. Paul Craddick
2095 Casey Hill Crescent
Grand Blanc, MI
48439

Dear Mr. Craddick:

Re: Order No. PSH-41529-3 – Sonic Sound Compact Micro-System

We regret to inform you that there will be a delay in shipping your order to you. The manufacturer has advised us that they can't keep up with demand for this new system and are consequently three (3) weeks behind in production.

As a result, we will not be able to process your order and ship your equipment to you until the week of July 10, 20xx. Once we ship it from here, it will take 3 to 5 days to reach you.

We apologize for this unfortunate delay. As a small token of our gratitude for your patience we are enclosing a $25 gift certificate that is valid at any one of our 158 retail stores across the country.

We appreciate your business and we will make every effort to ensure that your order gets shipped to you at the earliest possible date. If you have any questions about your order you can call our customer support line at 1-800-650-5500 and we will be happy to assist you.

Sincerely at your service,

Quenton Anderson
Manager, Mail Order Services

Order-Related: (delayed order notice)

(print Order-Related Letters on business letterhead paper)

July 17, 20xx

Mr. Ernie Comfort
165 Harlow Drive
Bangor, Maine
04401

Dear Mr. Comfort:

Re: Order No. PRT-619770-D7 – HP Color LaserJet 3600n Printer

We are sorry to inform you that there will be a slight delay in shipping the above-noted order to you. When we ran the Special Offer we were overwhelmed by orders and went through our on-hand inventory of this particular item within the first 24 hours.

However, we will be able to get this product to you very soon. We have checked with our supplier and they have plenty of units on hand in their warehouse. In order to expedite this product to you as soon as possible we have faxed the details of your order directly to the supplier who has agreed to drop ship the order directly to the ship-to address that you specified when you placed your telephone order.

As a result, you can expect to receive your order within 5 to 7 days of the date on this letter. So, when all is said and done your printer should arrive only about 5 days later than originally promised when you placed your order. Again, please accept our apologies.

We sincerely regret this unforeseen delay. We knew that we were making an excellent offer when we ran the Special, but we had no idea how strong the response would be. As a small token of gratitude for your patience we are enclosing a $25 printer cartridge refill certificate that will be honored anywhere HP printers are sold.

On behalf of Office Unlimited I would like to thank you for your continued patronage. If you have any questions about your order, please call our customer support line at 1-800-775-1292 and we will be happy to assist you.

Sincerely,

Liza Campanello
Customer Service Follow-Up

Order-Related: (order acknowledgement)

(print Order-Related Letters on business letterhead paper)

October 28, 20xx

Ms. Barbara Miller
P.O. Box 8084
Albany, NY 12209

Dear Barbara Miller:

Re: Your Order For "Instant Home Writing Kit"

I just received your mail order for *Instant Home Writing Kit*. Thanks very much. I'm sure you'll find that it will save you time and money doing your day-to-day writing work.

As you know (or as I believe you know), the Writing Kit is an eBook that you must download to your computer hard drive. It is not available in hardcopy form like a conventional book.

However, don't worry about that, because it is actually better than a regular book. Why? Because not only can you download it to your computer and read it online, you can also print it out and create your own hard copy. And that's not all. With this eBook you also receive a file of all of the letter and other document templates in the Kit that you can download straight into your word processing program (MS-Word compatible) and work with immediately.

That's right. Using one of the Kit's templates in your word processor, all you will have to do is copy, cut, and/or paste and you will have a ready-made professional looking letter in no time.

Barbara, I just need one thing from you now in order to get your Writing Kit to you – your e-mail address so I can send you the download link and instructions. Could you please send it to me by e-mail at findraft@sympatico.ca, or you can call me on my toll-free number at 1-800-600-6550.

I look forward to hearing from you soon.

Yours sincerely,

Robert Christian
President and Owner

Order-Related: (order confirmation)

(print Order-Related Letters on business letterhead paper)

February 17, 20xx

Mr. Noel Lansing
756 Horacio Drive
Albuquerque, NM 87111

Dear Mr. Lansing:

Re: Order No. 740299702 – TreadFast 979 Treadmill

The purpose of this is to confirm that your credit card payment has been approved and we will be shipping your new treadmill to you this week. Your order details are as follows:

> *One (1) TreadFast 979 Treadmill running machine, 2.5 HP with the following features: 0-10 MPH speed range, 24 in. x 80 in. walking belt, cushioned low-impact deck, gas-powered shock incline touch button adjustment system, built-in thumb pulse sensor, bottle/towel/remote holder, and 4 LCD displays for time, speed, distance, calories, pulse. One-year limited warranty.*

An amount of $999. has been charged to your credit card in the name of FitForLife Corporation.

Your order will be shipped to the above address by surface transport within the next three (3) days, and is guaranteed by the shipping company to arrive at destination within five (5) days of the shipping date.

If you have any questions about your order you can call our customer support line at 1-800-700-6700 and we will be happy to look after you.

Thanks for ordering from FitForLife Corporation.

Yours in fitness,

Miranda de Cruz
Fitness Consultant

Order-Related: (order fulfillment)

(print Order-Related Letters on business letterhead paper)

December 18, 20xx

Mrs. Brenda Erskine
5739 Sumner St.
Portland OR 97218

Dear Mrs. Erskine:

Re: Your Order - *Internet Basics Without Fear!* **– December 12, 20xx**

Thank you very much for your order of 24 copies of *Internet Basics Without Fear!* I'm so pleased that you chose it as the main reference text for your course "Introduction to the Internet for Seniors".

As a matter of fact, it was seniors that I had in mind specifically when I wrote the book. I had watched my 75-year old Father struggle to get online and I could see that it wasn't easy for him trying to work his way through all of the "techno-babble" in some of the so-called beginners books, even those "dummies" books.

As you requested, I have shipped the books via express courier so that you will receive them in time to prepare for your first sessions in early January.

The invoice is enclosed in a separate envelope inside the case of books, as you requested.

If you have any problems or questions, please don't hesitate to call me at my toll–free number, 1-800-600-6550.

Yours sincerely,

Robert Christian
President and Publisher

Order-Related: (partial order notice)

(print Order-Related Letters on business letterhead paper)

January 21, 20xx

Mr. Tom Myers
725 Spring Street
New York, NY 10012

Dear Mr. Myers:

Re: Order No. PSM-32547-7 – Sonic Sound Home Theatre System (5CD-DVD)

This is to advise you that we are sending the above-noted system to you by express courier today with one component missing, the remote control unit. The manufacturer has informed us that the remote control unit is on 3-week backorder status.

Nevertheless, since all of the functions of the system will operate using the manual controls, we felt it would be in your best interest to ship it to you right away while we await delivery of the remote unit.
The moment we receive the missing component we will ship it directly to you by super express courier service.

I trust that you will be in agreement with our decision to send the major components of your system to you right away rather than sitting in storage while we await the missing component.

If you have any questions about your order you can call our customer support line at 1-800-650-5500 and we will be happy to assist you.

Sincerely at your service,

Quenton Anderson
Manager, Mail Order Services

Order-Related: (product unavailable)

(print Order-Related Letters on business letterhead paper)

November 7, 20xx

Ms. Wendy Jamieson
78 Canal Center Road
Alexandria, VA
22314

Dear Ms. Jamieson:

Re: Your Order of "Business Writing Basics For Beginners"

I regret to advise you that the version of the book "Business Writing Basics For Beginners" (ISBN: 09684297-3-6) that you recently ordered is out of print and therefore no longer available.

However, you may be interested in the "revised" edition of this book (ISBN: 09684297-6-9) which we will be publishing next month. This new edition will be a little more expensive than the previous version, priced at $24.95 rather than $19.95. However, it will also include a lot more content, and will be completely up-to-date with the latest trends and conventions in business writing.

If you would like me to convert your existing order into one for the new version of the same title please call our toll free number at 1-800-645-5500 to confirm that change. If you do that we will immediately add your name to the "early bird" mailing list of people who will be sent the new book the week it comes off of the printing presses.

If you don't call to confirm we will assume that you have decided that you don't want the revised version of the book and we will simply cancel the original order.

Sincerely,

Caroline Smythe
Manager, Customer Orders

SALES AND MARKETING LETTERS

A business-to-customer "sales or marketing letter" is one that a company typically sends to all of its customers to announce and/or promote its products and/or services.

Typically, these types of letters deal with such things as new product announcements and special discount offers.

They are often sent as separate "mailers" but are sometimes included with other mailed items, such as invoices.

The following pages contain some typical real-life templates of business-to-customer sales and marketing letters.

Sales and Marketing Letters

Note On Template Size

Please note that the letter templates on the following pages have been reduced in size slightly from what I consider ideal so that they could fit onto single pages of this guide. Because of this, the top and bottom margins are wider than what is recommended for a standard business letter (see pg 45). In addition, a point size of 11 has been used rather than the ideal size of 12 points.

Sales and Marketing: (exclusive member mailer)

(print Sales Letter on product or corporate letterhead paper)

May 5, 20xx

To Member Mailing List
Member Address Line 2
Member Address Line 3
Member Address Line 4

Dear [member name],

       Special Offer – FREE Memberships For Your Family and/or Employees!

First,I would like to sincerely thank you for your patronage of CostRight Stores!

Second, in recognition of that loyal patronage, we have decided to make a valuable offer that you can pass on to your relatives and/or employees. An offer that we believe, they will be very happy to receive!

Our offer is this. From now until June 30, 20xx, your relatives and/or employees can become members at any CostRight Warehouse, simply by filling out the enclosed pre-approved registration forms. No strings attached!

By joining, these relatives and/or employees will be receiving at no charge, the equivalent of a CostRight Privileged Membership, which has a value of $50 per year, plus taxes. This type of membership includes eligibility for a free Spouse card, as well (see Passport document enclosed).

In addition, if they become CostRight members right away, your relatives and/or employees will also qualify for their own Passport that will make them eligible for more than $1,500 in additional savings on various products over the summer months. These special discounts are being offered exclusively to CostRight Members by our suppliers.

By passing on this offer and giving these pre-approved membership applications to your relatives and/or employees, you will be allowing them to obtain many summer products at near-cost prices, as well as making them eligible for many other CostRight benefits. And it won't cost you anything!

Why not give your relatives and/or employees a chance to receive all of the benefits of a CostRight Membership? Not only will they very much appreciate the many savings that you give them, but they will also remember your generous gift every time they make a purchase this summer!

What do you have to lose?

Thank you for your kind consideration.

Sandra Brunette
Manager, Membership Programs

P.S.
If you run out of pre-approved membership applications, please don't hesitate to call us at (416) 274-3572 and we will look after your needs right away.

Encl.

Sales and Marketing: (personalized sales letter)

(print Sales Letter on product or corporate letterhead)

May 3, 20xx

Mr. Rob Cunningham
President, Cunningham Racing
89 Newton Drive, Suite 507
Toledo, OH 43612

Dear Mr. Cunningham:

It was nice chatting with you briefly on the telephone earlier today. As I said, it was Dan Borhman who does the marketing work for Tae-Box who suggested I call you. Dan and I are now involved in final discussions aimed at getting the Tae-Box logo placed on our new drug awareness product right beside D.A.R.T.'s. During my last chat with Dan, he suggested I give you a call because of your involvement in the health and fitness club business and your personal interest in Tae-Box.

Enclosed for your review is our new drug awareness poster entitled *"The Self-Destructive Use of Drugs"*. This unique and internationally acclaimed educational product has taken the International Drug Awareness Research Foundation (IDARI) more than two years to research, develop, test and perfect. IDARI is currently on a mission to distribute this powerful communications tool across North America.

The primary purpose of *"The Self-Destructive Use of Drugs"* is to inform and educate: kids, parents, teachers, coaches, legislators, clergy, military personnel, healthcare professionals, law enforcement officials, business and community leaders, and many others, about the factual and objective truth related to the use and abuse of all drugs, both legal and illegal. As you can see, it very graphically demonstrates the *"mind-body-drug connection"* involving all of the major drug groups.

Just imagine the impact that this poster will have once it is hung on the walls of every school, home, community center, health/fitness club, workshop, police station, clubhouse, lunch room, medical clinic, sports facility, hospital, doctor's office, dentist's office, barracks, library, etc., throughout North America? We believe that the wide-spread dissemination of *"The Self-Destructive Use of Drugs"* will significantly increase substance abuse awareness and prevention, especially among kids.

One feature of the poster that I thought would interest Cunningham Racing is its promotional aspect. We have designed it so that an organization's name, logo and/or message can be custom-printed at the bottom of the poster. This is a very powerful way for an organization to send a compelling prevention message, while at the same time giving them a high level of recognition and visibility.

I can already visualize your slogan *"Don't Let Anything Stand In The Way Of Your Dream"* custom-printed on the bottom of this high-visibility and attention-grabbing wall hanging (Your slogan is perfect for inclusion on a drug awareness poster!). This would definitely be a powerful communications vehicle that you could distribute widely throughout your network of health and fitness clubs.

I trust you will still see the powerful marketing opportunity here. I therefore look forward to hearing from you soon about how you might use this product. I can be reached in Montreal at (514) 979-1298.

Sincerely,

Brian R. Casey, M.B.A.
Vice-President, Marketing and Communications

Sales and Marketing: (product sales mailer)

(print Sales Letter on product or corporate letterhead)

November 1, 20xx

Eliminate Writer's Block Forever!

Dear [Customer Name]:

If you've ever struggled with everyday writing tasks, the *INSTANT WRITING HELP KIT!* is made for you. Instead of having to go through that painful process of sitting in front of a blank screen with a blank mind (a feeling that most of us know all too well), we have developed a product that **will kick-start the writing process for you.**

In day-to-day life most of us are frequently confronted by important **"must do" writing tasks** which we'd rather not do. I'm talking about writing normal everyday things like: recommendation letters, resignation letters, letters of complaint, sales and marketing letters, thank you letters, and on and on. Then there are the more **complex writing tasks** such as: resumes and CVs, cover letters, speeches, application form texts, newsletter articles, etc.

The fact is, **most of us aren't writers.** We run our lives and businesses, that's what we do first and foremost. Of course, we can always try to farm the job out to someone else, but that is often a problem because these little writing jobs usually require our personal input due to specific knowledge that only we possess. Not only that, but most people will charge us by the hour for each and every writing job. **Hiring others can get expensive (i.e. $60 to $100 per hour).**

INSTANT WRITING HELP KIT! has been designed to let you **do those necessary writing tasks yourself** in a matter of a few minutes. It provides you with literally dozens of examples of just about any type of day-to-day correspondence that you can think of. Each sample template is based on a real-life situation that you will identify with, and that you will be able to easily **adapt to your own personal situation in a matter of minutes.**

Perhaps you need to write a complaint letter to your telephone company. Maybe it's a short speech that you have to give at your sister's wedding. What about updating your resume or c.v. and drafting a good cover letter for that job you just saw advertised?

INSTANT WRITING HELP KIT! will be there to make it easy for you. With scores of examples, and templates that you can adapt to your own situation in just a few short minutes.

You Won't Have To Suffer From Writer's Block Ever Again!

INSTANT WRITING HELP KIT! will make your life easier. It will also save you money. And it's **only $29.95** for the complete kit! You'll save this much writing your very first letter with *INSTANT WRITING HELP KIT!*

To order *INSTANT WRITING HELP KIT!* today, call **1-800-600-6550.**

Wishing you success,

Robert Christian

P.S.
Order now and you will receive a **Free Bonus Book** on how to optimize your time on the Internet!

Sales and Marketing: (leave behind letter)

(print Sales Letter on product or corporate letterhead)

Date: _____

_____
_____
_____
_____

Dear _____ :

YOU Can Make A Very Important Difference!

Unfortunately, when I dropped in at your office I wasn't able to meet with you in person. Since it was not essential that I see you personally, I am leaving this brief letter to explain why I came to visit.

I represent a non-profit organization called the International Drug Awareness Research Institute. IDARI's sole purpose is to develop and distribute drug awareness information products. I have recently been canvassing small businesses in your area in search of socially concerned business people who would like to sponsor one or more copies of our internationally acclaimed drug awareness poster *"The Self-Destructive Use of Drugs*. Since I wasn't able to meet with you personally, I have taken the liberty of leaving a copy of that poster for your review and consideration.

This poster provides all of the essential information about the mind-body-drug connection, all in one place, presented in an arresting, factual, and non-judgmental way. The Foundation's primary mission is to distribute the poster's life-saving message as widely as possible throughout communities across North America. As you are probably aware, the first critical step in tackling the substance abuse problem is through increasing the level of drug awareness in our communities. Can you imagine the impact that this poster will have once it is hanging in every school, medical clinic, community center, hospital, doctor's office, place of worship, and workplace, in this one community alone?

It is in the context of this kind of community spirit that we are appealing to your social conscience to consider purchasing one or more copies of *"The Self-Destructive Use of Drugs*" to be displayed in the office or work area of your company. Making a donation like this to such a worthy and compelling cause would definitely be a strong statement on your part as to where you and/or your business stand on drug awareness and education.

With the poster, I have left some background materials, plus an invoice for payment. ***Should you wish to keep the poster, would you please complete and return the attached invoice/order form with your payment (or call us to pick-up your order).*** There is absolutely no obligation. If you decide that you do not want to purchase the poster, for whatever reason, I would ask you to please call me at the number listed below and I will pick-up the poster as soon as possible.

Trusting that you will choose to help us carry the drug awareness message.

Yours sincerely,

_____   _____
Community Liaison Representative   Tel. No.

Sales and Marketing: (solicit former customer)

(print Sales Letter on product or corporate letterhead)

May 5, 20xx

Mr. Donald Medland
650 East Huronia Ave.
Apartment 1505
Chicago, IL 60611

Dear Mr. Medland,

We're Back At the Front of the Pack and We Want You Back!

My name is Ron Armstrong and I am the newly appointed Manager of Marketing and Customer Relations here at Software Solutions Inc. My very first priority in my new position is to contact a few key former SSI customers such as you, to see if we can persuade you to take a fresh look at what we have to offer since our company was restructured.

It's no secret that Software Solutions went through a very difficult period for a couple of years. Unfortunately, some of the internal pressures in the company at that time resulted in a rapid decline in customer service and new product development. As I understand it, that situation had a lot to do with you choosing to take your business elsewhere 18 months ago.

Well I'm happy to tell you that all of that is behind us now and we're back on track at SSI!

As it turns out, this period of difficulty has resulted in an opportunity for us which not many companies ever have. By necessity, we were forced to review our entire operation and product line from the ground up, and the results have been amazing! We've now learned how to develop products "outside of the box".

In addition, as you might have read in the business press, SSI has a new owner with very deep pockets. This has allowed us to invest more resources in new product development than ever before. I'm sure you'll be impressed with the results.

We have also adopted a "best in class" management philosophy which means that we now constantly benchmark the competition and make it our specific goal to keep one step ahead of what the others are doing. That's what our latest release of eCommerce solutions software is all about. We've one-upped the competition once again, just like we used to do during our first few years of existence.

Yes, we're definitely back on track.

I will be contacting you personally next week to tell you more about our exciting new generation of products, and to tell you everything that we are willing to do to get your business back.

I look forward to talking with you.

Yours sincerely,

Ron Armstrong
Manager, Marketing and Customer Relations

Sales and Marketing: (targeted customer mailer)

(print Sales Letter on product or corporate letterhead)

October 25, 20xx

To Trainer Mailing List
Trainer Address Line 2
Trainer Address Line 3
Trainer Address Line 4

Dear [name of training professional]:

This Book Is Both a Training and a Marketing Tool!

According to the latest surveys, at least 60% of the North American population are not yet Internet-friendly. All of these people are your potential customers. Our research continues to unquestionably confirm that a very large percentage of the "ordinary" people out there are still avoiding the Net due to the barrier of technology (whether real or perceived) that still has them frightened off. *Internet Basics without fear!* was designed and written with those people expressly in mind.

Help the Baby-Boomers Get Online!

Remember, the large majority of "baby boomers" were not brought up using computers. It is these people, the group now between 35 and 55 years old – with 2/3 of the disposable income - that have not yet migrated to the Internet as much as the younger age groups. Our research has shown that *Internet Basics without fear!* has immense appeal for those boomers. Without fail, these people relate to the simple, straightforward approach of this book and see it as their entry point to the World Wide Web.

A Powerful Training and Marketing Tool For You!

With its very accessible user-friendly and non-technical approach, *Internet Basics without fear!* is an ideal training tool, as well as a vehicle for connecting you with those hundreds of thousands of potential customers who you haven't been able to reach yet. You could use this book as a training tool and/or a marketing and sales vehicle, in any one of a number of ways:

- As an advertising promotion; offering potential customers a free copy of the book with their purchase of a training course or other products or services;
- As a value-added part of your basic training package; for use as a course training tool;
- As a low-cost premium to existing customers for a nominal fee - or perhaps at no charge - in exchange for them ordering additional training services;
- As a bonus familiarization premium for non-technical employees in your organization;
- As a promotional tool for your business with a customized corporate logo or sticker on the cover.

These are just a few ways that you could use *Internet Basics without fear!* to attract new customers and grow your business. Information for ordering copies of this powerful training and marketing tool is contained in the enclosed brochure. A quantity discount schedule is available on request.

Yours in customer service,

Robert Christian

Encl.

OTHER BUSINESS-TO-CUSTOMER LETTERS

These are miscellaneous business-to-customer letters that don't fall clearly into any one of the other major business-to-customer categories.

The following pages contain real-life templates of various uncategorized business-to-customer letters.

Other Business-to-Customer Letters

Note On Template Size

Please note that the letter templates on the following pages have been reduced in size slightly from what I consider ideal so that they could fit onto single pages of this guide. Because of this, the top and bottom margins are wider than what is recommended for a standard business letter (see pg 45). In addition, a point size of 11 has been used rather than the ideal size of 12 points.

Announcement: (new location)

(print Announcement Letter on business letterhead paper)

February 26, 20xx

To Customer List
Customer Address Line 2
Customer Address Line 3
Customer Address Line 4

Dear [Customer Name]:

We're Opening On The Other Side Of Town!

And we can hardly wait!

As you might already know if you have visited our west-end store or have watched the commercials on the WCAV Dinner Time News program lately, Donnelly's Stereo Center will be opening its brand new store in the east-end of town on Wednesday March 5, 20xx.

The new store is located on Dynes Road just across form the train station, next to McDonald's.

The Grand Opening festivities will begin at 9:00 a.m.. There will be entertainment for the whole family and loads of "freebies" for all. The Crazy Aces Comedy Troupe will be there to keep the kids busy while you check out our new digs, and child care services will be available. We'll be serving free coffee and soft drinks throughout the day, and if you get there soon enough there might even be some homemade cookies left!

Of course, everything in the store will be on sale at specially reduced prices. In addition to a number of Grand Opening Home Entertainment Package Deals, everything in the store will be marked down by at least 20%. Some items will be discounted by as much as 40%. This sale will only be on for three days, so make sure you don't miss it!

And, just so you don't forget about our other location, we will be offering a "Cross Town Special". Any purchase that you make at the new store of $250 or more during the Grand Opening Sale will qualify you for an automatic 20% discount off the regular price of any item at our west-end location, as long as that purchase is made within 5 days of your Grand Opening sale purchase. See the in-store flyer for more details.

Please come out and join us for fun and bargains as we celebrate our new location!

In celebration!

Frank Gamble
President and CEO

Apology: (customer service error)

(print Apology Letter on business letterhead paper)

June 28, 20xx

Ms. Rebecca Quinlan
2595 Dewhurst Circle
Unit No. 16
Birmingham, AL 35233

Dear Ms. Quinlan:

The purpose of this is to convey to you my sincere apologies for any inconvenience you may have experienced last month with respect to the installation of your Internet high speed service.

I just returned from vacation this week and found your file in my in-basket. As soon as I reviewed your case it was clear that somehow your May 20th request for a change in service had somehow slipped through the cracks. The only possible explanation I can give is that we have recently had a number of key staff changes which might have resulted in your letter being overlooked.

Consequently, I have directed our Installation Group to contact you by the end of this week to set up a time convenient to you when they could go to your house and install your new router and make the necessary adjustments to your software.

Because of this serious oversight, and as a testament to our appreciation to you as our customer, we are going to provide you with your first three months of high speed service free of charge. Therefore, your account will not be billed until October of this year.

Ms. Quinlan, let me assure you that what happened in your case is not typical of CableNet's level of customer service. We continue to be committed to providing you and all of our customers with the highest standards of service in the industry.

If you have any questions please don't hesitate to call me at 754-9785.

Yours in service,

Paulo Colanzi
Manager, Customer Solutions

Condolence: (long-time customer)

(ideally, Letters of Condolence should be hand-written)

November 16, 20xx

2698 Stonehearst Ave.
Toronto, ON
H4S 7Y6

Dear Robert:

I would like to express my sincere condolences on the recent passing of your father. Veronica and the children also send their thoughts and prayers to you and your family at this difficult time.

I can still picture in my mind's eye, that day over 30 years ago, when your Dad brought you into the store for the first time. You got so excited when he bought you that 10-speed racer I was afraid you were going to hurt yourself when you charged out into the parking lot. You should have seen the smile on your Dad's face as you raced off for home! He was one proud father.

As I believe you are aware, your Dad and I grew up together and went to the same high school. Later, his young family became my valued customers. Over the years, I saw your father grow into a hard working and highly respected member of this community. When the two of us worked together on various community projects, I was often in awe of his truly caring nature and the great kindness and compassion he extended to those less fortunate than himself. I know that his good works changed the lives of many in this town.

He will be missed by all of us. You were truly fortunate to have such a man as a model in your life.

As you know, it was not that long ago that my own father passed away, so I have some idea of what you and your family are going through. No sentiment of comfort is quite enough to replace the loss.

Please pass on my deepest sympathies to your mother, and brother, and sister, and to all of your father's grandchildren.

Sincere sympathy,

Jack Hutchinson

Congratulations: (former employee)

(print Letter of Congratulations on business letterhead paper)

March 25, 20xx

Belinda Asher
620 Mayview Ave.
Pineville, WV
24874

Dear Belinda:

On behalf of everyone here at Deerwood Resorts Ltd., I would like to sincerely congratulate you on your recent graduation from Mountain State University with your M.B.A. (Marketing).

I must say that I was not surprised to read of your success in the newspaper. During your first of four summers as an employee at our Lakeland Family Resort I noted how bright you are and how you have a very quick mind for business. Combine those attributes with your relentless work ethic and commitment to quality customer service, and it is obvious that you have a wide-open future ahead of you. I can only hope that your experience working with us contributed in some small way to your success.

On behalf of the management and staff at Deerwood Resorts I wish you all the best in your future career and life endeavors, whatever they may be.

Yours sincerely,

Bruce Atkinson
President and CEO

Follow-Up: (after conference contact)

(print Follow-Up Letter on company letterhead paper)

June 29, 20xx

Edward Patterson
Vice President, Sales
Global Thermodynamics Inc.
4500 - 97 West Avenue SE
Edmonton, Alberta
T2C 2L8

Dear Ed:

It was great meeting you and getting to know a little bit about both you and Global Thermodynamics at last week's Global Petroleum Show in Calgary. It was the biggest trade show I have ever attended. I trust that you found it very beneficial as well.

Please let me tell you a bit more about our company. Logistica Inc. is a specialized logistics and third party transportation management company, based in Edmonton. It is an independent service provider committed to improving logistics operating efficiencies for shippers such as your company. I would ask you to please take a few minutes to browse our Website to find out more about our company and the services we offer. (http://logistica.ca).

Ed, I truly believe that Logistica will bring you economically sound logistics solutions.

We look forward to quoting on your shipping requirements. Please drop me a line or give me a call whenever you would like us to prepare a quotation for you. I can be reached in Edmonton at 406-275-7357 or by e-mail at fred@logistica.ca.

Yours sincerely,

Fred Tarnhower, PMP
President and Owner
Logistica Inc.

Follow-Up: (after in-store contact)

(print Sales Follow-Up Letter on company letterhead paper)

March 15, 20xx

Ms. Wendy Todd
891 Fourth Ave.
Ann Arbor, MI 48104

Dear Ms. Todd:

This is just a quick follow-up note to thank you for dropping in at Downtown Toyota and entering our "Miles of Smiles" contest. Your entry has been processed and is entered in the draw which will take place on April 10, 20xx.

I enjoyed our brief chat about the various models of Toyota cars that might be of interest to you. Your observation about the low interest rates we are offering on our lease financing was absolutely correct. As you said, it is the period of economic prosperity the economy is now experiencing that allows us to offer such low rates.

As I mentioned, when the time comes for you to trade in your current vehicle, I would be very pleased to brief you on the entire line of Toyota passenger vehicles so that you will be able to make an informed decision about which vehicle best suits your needs. Any time you would like to discuss your personal transportation needs, please give me a call at 234-7865.

In the meantime, I would ask you to please accept the enclosed key chain as a small token of your visit to Downtown Toyota and your entry into the "Miles for Smiles" draw.

At your service,

David Chen
Senior Sales Associate

Enclosure (1)

Fundraising: (community project)

(print Fundraising Letter on company letterhead paper)

November 30, 20xx

To Customer List
Customer Address Line 2
Customer Address Line 3
Customer Address Line 4

Dear [Customer Name]:

Will You Join Me In Protecting Our Community?

I am sending this to you as a fellow member of the Pinewood Acres community. I'm sure that you must value living in such a quiet and peaceful neighborhood, just like I do.

You know, sometimes in order to keep one's community "quiet and peaceful" one has to take action. That's what this letter is about – taking action – community action.

By now, via media reports and word of mouth you must be aware of the significant increase in house break-ins in this neighborhood over the past couple of years. In fact, the break-in rate has more than doubled over the past two years. According to the police this is just a sign of the times as the economic downturn continues and local businesses and factories continue to close their doors for good.

As you may know, a local Community Action Committee has been meeting over the past two months to try to find ways to reduce the break-in rate in Pinewood Acres. Last week they released their recommendations on how best to combat that problem. Their primary recommendation calls for increased police and security patrols to supplement the local Neighborhood Watch program. They estimate that the extra cost to double nighttime (after dark) security patrols by Secure Inc. will be in the range of $15,000 to $20,000 per year. Unfortunately, this amount is not included in this year's municipal budget allocation and there are no additional funds available.

Therefore, as a concerned member of this community I have decided that my business will take the lead in assisting with this year's security control budget. Accordingly, Branscombe's Hardare will donate $1 for every $2 raised in the community to cover the additional security costs.

I urge you to join me today in supporting this worthy cause for our common good. To make your donation today you can drop in to either one of our two stores and deposit your donation in the boxes provided near the front cashes. If you can't make it to the store, please send a check or money order, made out to "CAC Security Patrol" and mail it to the address listed at the top of this letter.

Together, we can make sure that Pinewood Acres continues to be "a better place to live".

Yours in community spirit,

Gerry Cartwright
President and Owner

Reference: (former customer)

(print Credit Reference Letter on company letterhead paper)

April 21, 20xx

To Whom It May Concern:

Credit Reference: Mr. Paulo Renzetti

This is to confirm that Mr. Paulo Renzetti has been a regular customer of good standing with Maximum Merchandise since 1995.

During that 10-year period Mr. Renzetti was one of our credit card holders. He made purchases from our stores on a regular basis and has an impeccable record of making regular payments on time. In fact, according to our credit database records, during the entire period that Mr. Renzetti was our regular customer he was never once late in making a payment. This is exceptional in the credit business.

Accordingly, based on our experience with Mr. Renzetti as one of our most valued credit card customers for over 10 years, I am pleased to recommend him as a highly dependable and extremely low credit risk.

If you require further information, please feel free to call me at (416) 450-9800.

Sincerely,

Margaret Miller
Customer Credit Manager

Thank You: (customer survey participation)

(print Thank You Letter on company letterhead paper)

March 25, 20xx

Mr. Bernard Armstrong
120 Nicholson Road, No. 505
Newmarket, ON
L3Y 7V1

Dear Mr. Armstrong:

Customer Preference Survey – Your Participation Gift

I would like to personally thank you for participating in our recent survey of customer preferences related to your purchase of office supplies and equipment.

You were one of an elite group of 100 of our most valuable customers who were hand-picked to participate in the survey. We wanted to know about the unique preferences of our very best customers when it comes to both products and services offered by Office Essentials. Your input will be valuable to us as we continue to develop and implement our one-to-one "customer preference program". Over the next few months you will start noticing the implementation of new programs and strategies that resulted directly from survey feedback.

As promised when you signed up, in appreciation for your participation in the survey we would like to offer you a special gift. Enclosed you will find a merchandise gift certificate for $50 that can be redeemed against the purchase of any product or service offered by Office Essentials at any one of our 87 retail outlets nationwide.

We thank you for your ongoing support of Office Essentials and we look forward to a continued relationship with you based on high quality products and services backed by unsurpassed customer service.

Yours sincerely,

Les Woods
Manager, Customer Service Programs

Encl.

THIRD EDITION – NEW LETTER TEMPLATES

For the Third Edition of *Instant Business Letter Kit* I have added an additional 29 real-life letter business letter templates. These are additional letters that I developed for various business situations/customers since the last version of the Kit was published.

They include an assortment of both business-to-business letters and business-to-customer letters as listed below:

Employee Letters (pg. 199)

Employee – Welcome New Staff After Merger
Employee – Quarterly Report To Staff
Employee – Training Extension
Employee – Letter of Reference
Employee – Letter of Commendation
Employee – Goodbye to Co-workers

Business Proposal Letters (pg. 207)

Proposal – Business Service Partnership
Proposal – Academic Partnership
Proposal – Special Event

Project and Contract Letters (pg. 211)

Project – Letter of Interest
Project – Letter of Credit
Contract – Expedite Payment Request
Contract – Provide Background Information
Contract – Notice of Audit
Contract – Cancellation Notice

Marketing and Promotion Letters (pg. 219)

Marketing and Promotion – Promote Small Business
Marketing and Promotion – Promote New Referral Program
Marketing and Promotion – Announce New Program

Recommendation Letters (pg. 223)

Recommendation – Business Colleague
Recommendation – Business Associate
Recommendation – Employee Travel Visa

Financial Hardship Letters (pg. 229)

Financial Hardship – Consolidate and Restructure Debt
Financial Hardship – Provide Background Information
Financial Hardship – Request For Short Sale

Condolence and Sympathy Letters (pg. 233)

Condolence – To Brother of Deceased
Sympathy – To Family of Deceased
Sympathy - To Spouse of Deceased

Other Business Letters (pg. 237)

Other Letters – Customer Appreciation
Other Letters – Proposal Cover Letter

For more **business-to-business** letters see the Second Edition letters on **page 71.**

For more **business-to-customer** letters see the Second Edition letters on **page 141.**

Note On Template Size

Please note that the letter templates on the following pages have been reduced in size slightly from what I consider ideal so that they could fit onto single pages of this guide. Because of this, the top and bottom margins are wider than what is recommended for a standard business letter (see pg 45). In addition, a point size of 11 has been used rather than the ideal size of 12 points.

EMPLOYEE LETTERS

A business-to-business "employee letter" is an internal company business letter. Typically it is a letter that a company sends to one of its employees to advise the person of various matters related to their employment status with the company.

The following pages contain real-life templates of the most common internal business-to-business employee letters.

Please take note. Since employee letters are "internal" business letters, many of them can also be written in the form of an internal corporate memorandum. Accordingly, the following templates include examples of both letter and memo formats.

Employee Letters

Employee – Welcome New Staff After Merger (pg. 200)
Employee – Quarterly Report To Staff (pg. 201)
Employee – Training Extension (pg. 202)
Employee – Letter of Reference (pg. 203)
Employee – Letter of Commendation (pg. 204)
Employee – Goodbye to Co-workers (pg. 205)

To see some other Employee Letters go to page 79.

Note On Template Size

Please note that the letter templates on the following pages have been reduced in size slightly from what I consider ideal so that they could fit onto single pages of this guide. Because of this, the top and bottom margins are wider than what is recommended for a standard business letter (see pg 45). In addition, a point size of 11 has been used rather than the ideal size of 12 points.

Employee: (welcome new staff after merger)

(print Letter to Staff on corporate letterhead paper)

November 15, 20xx

To: All New Team Members - DRS Team-India - New Delhi, India

Dear DRS Team-India Members:

Subject: Welcome To The DRS Family!

Please let me start by sincerely welcoming each and every one of you to the Dynamic Real-Estate Systems (DRS) team. I am extremely excited about extending our company to include you at DRS Team-India!

I believe that when you decided to join DRS it was a forward looking career move that you won't regret. I know you all have varying degrees of knowledge about our company so I'll just highlight a few key points below to bring you all up to speed:

- DRS is a major division of American Systems Group, Inc., a nationwide - U.S.A. - company with superior financial ratios, a proven track record of being profitable every single year, combined with more than 17 years of continued growth in the information management systems development and operation business.

- DRS is known as a leader in the real-estate software industry in the U.S.A. and currently has offices in 15 states, with more to follow by the end of this year. The company is guided by a team of seasoned managers who collectively possess more than 80 years of experience in the IT and systems development industries.

- While many of our competitors have been struggling over the past few years, DRS continues to show significant growth; enabled by a highly productive sales and operations team coupled with innovative leading-edge technology platforms, processes, and systems that give us the competitive edge.

I believe that the decision we made a few months ago to set up DRS Team-India is an exciting and innovative strategy that fits perfectly with our business operations in the Los Angeles area. With the daily hand-off of files-in-process from DRS Team-USA to DRS Team-India we will be poised to significantly increase our overall productivity by as much as 50% once we are operating at full speed.

I am convinced that a large measure of DRS's success to date is because of its commitment to its people. When I speak of our focus being on people here I am referring to both our employees AND our key customers and agents across the United States who deliberately choose to do business with us.

To all of our DRS team members, we offer a business environment and culture that provides: career path advancement, leading-edge and innovative technology platforms, rewards for exceptional performance, and empowerment and promotion from within. To our valuable and loyal customers, we strive to do everything in our power to "exceed our customers expectations" and to always deliver that magical "wow factor" that will keep them coming back for more.

In closing, I just want to reaffirm how thrilled the entire DRS team here in the Los Angeles area office is that DRS Team-India will be up and running and adding extra value to the products and services we offer to our clients. Together, I am convinced that we can take DRS to that next level of success.

Looking forward to personally meeting each and every one of you soon!

Yours sincerely,

Brad Grainger
President

Employee: (quarterly report to staff)

(print Letter to Staff on corporate letterhead paper)

October 18, 20xx

To All Staff - DRS Offices Worldwide

Re: Third Quarter Update – 20xx

A lot has happened since my last quarterly update that I am optimistic about.

Even though it was the traditionally slow summer vacation period, we managed to maintain our overall sales volume levels. I am very encouraged by this because I see it as more evidence of a pattern of consistency that has been emerging that demonstrates that we are capable of sustaining our performance levels over time, in spite of seasonal and cyclical market fluctuations.

In addition, we already have a number of initiatives underway or planned that I believe will allow us to be even more productive and better than ever at "exceeding our customers expectations".

* I am excited and optimistic about our establishment of DRS Team-India in late September. The daily hand-off of files-in-process from DRS Team-USA to DRS Team-India should significantly reduce average sales processing and contract drawing times. There are plans to add additional tasks to DRS Team-India which will further provide a major competitive advantage over all of our competitors. Related to this last point, I want to thank all of those on Team-USA who offered an unconditional "yes" when asked if they would be willing to visit our operation in India to provide training and team building assistance.

* DRS continues to invest heavily in both capital and time in developing technology-based automation tools and systems that will streamline our operations and improve our productivity at all levels so that we can continually offer our agents innovative products and services. When fully implemented, the multiple modules of our new DRS ePower automated sales and follow-up system will give us a powerful and robust technology platform that will seamlessly adjust to meet our increasing support and service needs as we grow and expand our operations over time.

* In addition to the ongoing and organic growth of our current operations, we are now considering the possibility of making some targeted acquisitions of small IT sales and service operations. These will be strategic acquisitions of companies with business models and cultures that mesh with those of DRS, and they will be in geographical locations that are also compatible with our operations.

Between now and the end of this year we will continue to develop innovative technology platforms designed to further streamline our operations and enhance the products and services that we offer our customers. In fact, I believe that our ongoing efforts to continuously improve the products, services and pricing mix that we offer to both our customers and our agents will be a never-ending quest if we are to stay at the forefront of our industry.

Thanks for your help in achieving another great quarter for DRS. We continue to make steady and encouraging progress towards our $5 million per month target. I have no doubts that if we continue to work as a team committed to exceeding our customers expectations we will move ever closer to that goal.

Yours sincerely,

Brad Grainger
President

Employee: (training extension)

(print Employee Extension Letter on corporate letterhead paper)

December 15, 20xx

Mr. Randall Swift
Director, International Law Programs
International Law Foundation
2550 Washington Ave., Suite 1055
Washington, D.C. 20105

Dear Mr. Swift:

Subject: Training Period Extension – Jason Radner

The purpose of this letter is to request a six month extension of Jason Radner's training period. I am an attorney and partner at Thompson & Peet LLP., and I am writing this as Mr. Radner's supervisor during his assignment to our firm as an international trainee.

Jason's current training period is scheduled to end on January 15th, 20xx. As you know, this training program was designed especially to help him engage in the full time practice of general corporate law. His performance so far in his training program has been excellent, and he has made rapid progress through all of his assigned tasks.

To develop into a successful corporate lawyer, Jason must not only master the field of general corporate law; he also needs to master different specialized areas of related law, particularly in the fields of Banking Law, Finance Law, and Bankruptcy Law. Because of his success to-date in general corporate law, our firm would be pleased to provide Jason with the entire skill-set necessary to become a complete corporate law specialist. We believe that he requires this extended training if he is to become a well-rounded corporate lawyer ready to navigate his way upward in his career, fully prepared to meet the challenges that lie ahead of him.

In addition, during his extended stay at our firm, I would have the opportunity to train Jason on how to identify the industry and/or specific types of business transactions that interest him the most, and then expose him to work on as many of those types of transactions as possible. The more he works in the context of a particular industry or transaction type, the better position he will be in to understand the relevant business objectives and issues.

In closing, I urge you to agree to a six-month extension of Jason Radner's training period so that I can complete the training already begun that will give him the full set of skills and knowledge he will need to become a successful corporate lawyer. Please do not hesitate to contact me if you would like to discuss this further.

Sincerely,

Jessica Franklin
Partner

Employee (letter of reference)

(print Employee Reference Letter on corporate letterhead paper)

January 10, 20xx

Addressee Line 1
Addressee Line 2
Addressee Line 3
Addressee Line 4

To Whom It May Concern:

Subject: Reference Letter – Charles Dawson

I am very pleased to write this letter of reference on behalf of Charles Dawson in my capacity as CFO of Longview, Inc., Longview is a recent start-up Web Services development company that specializes in providing hosting, networking and ancillary services to the corporate sector. Overall, I believe Charles to be a skilled, thoughtful, and thoroughly professional Information Technology expert, which I will briefly elaborate on below.

I have known Charles as one of my key employees for almost three years. I first got to know him when he helped us develop a software system as a Research Assistant in Computer Science Department at the University of Illinois. On that project I was impressed by his initiative and his thirst for knowledge. He also showed strong analytical and problem solving skills. In fact, it was for those qualities that we hired him at Longview, Inc. after his graduation in September, 20xx.

During the almost three years that Charles has worked with me at Longview Inc., I have always been impressed by his outstanding diligence and his high level of technical expertise. Indeed, I have been more than satisfied with our working relationship. During this period, I also had the great pleasure of watching him blossom from a junior software developer into a fully functioning business-oriented Principal Software Architect who played the primary architecture and software management role on some of our company's key projects. I was particularly impressed by the professionalism and technical innovation that Richard demonstrated on our Tandem Network Project.

Not only is Charles highly intelligent; he also is very hard-working. He has tackled every project assigned to him with enthusiasm and competence. He invariably understands exactly what a project is all about from the outset, and how to get it done quickly and effectively. He consistently produces superior quality work, on time, and within budget targets. In my estimation, Charles is a true example of the type of employee that every employer wants: accountable and responsible, with a superior work ethic and a high degree of integrity.

In closing, I recommend Charles Dawson very highly for any position in the IT field that involves complexity and creativity, with high quality requirements. He is an exceptionally bright and hardworking person who will do his very best to do an outstanding job for whomever he works. If I may be of further assistant with regard to Charles, please call me at xxx-xxx-xxxx or e-mail me at xxxxxxxxxx.

Sincerely,

Dennis Stafford, Ph.D.
Professor of Finance, University of Illinois
CFO, Longview, Inc.

Employee (letter of commendation)

(print Letter of Commendation on corporate letterhead stationery)

January 12, 20xx

Ms. Rita Gonzalez
Managing Director
Marketing and Communications
The Evanston Agency
1500 Congress, Ste. 750
Austin, TX 78701

Dear Ms. Gonzalez:

Re: Commendation - Shannon Berloitz

The purpose of this letter is to formally and publicly commend Shannon Berloitz for the excellent service she provided to Target-Track Inc. throughout the ramp-up and launch of our new product line. In my opinion, the level of service that Ms. Berloitz extended to our company was far beyond our expectations.

I have never before written a letter like this on an entirely unsolicited basis. However, in this case I was so impressed by the support and service provided by Ms.Berloitz and her small team of marketing and communications specialists that I felt compelled to go on record with my praise. These people truly deserve it. In an era where exceptional one-to-one customer service excellence has virtually disappeared from our industry, the work that Shannon and her team did should be held up as an example for others to try to emulate.

What particularly impressed me about the level of service provided by Ms. Berloitz et al was that there were no additional financial rewards involved. It appears that it was simply the team's extraordinary commitment to excellence in customer service and support that motivated them to always go the extra mile. Their example even had a positive impact on the attitude and productivity of our own staff!

In closing, I believe that Shannon Berloitz and her team truly deserve to be congratulated and rewarded for providing customer service and support well beyond the expectations of our company on the Target-Track project.

Very sincerely,

David Humphries
Vice-President, Business Development

Employee: (goodbye to co-workers)

(print Employee Goodbye Letter to co-workers on corporate letterhead)

August 12, 20xx

Dear Friends:

As a number of you already know I have recently accepted a position with another company and will be leaving at the end of this week. Please consider this to be my sincere goodbye to each and every one of you.

I want you all to know that I am truly leaving here with mixed feelings; happy about my new career opportunity, but sad to be leaving such a great company where I have so many wonderful friends and colleagues. The last three years as a member of the SysTek team was the best period of my career so far. I learned a great deal and worked with many people with whom I am sure I will remain friends for a long time. I can only wish that my new job will give me such rewarding experiences and supportive friends.

Thank you so much for making my time at SysTek a truly enjoyable one. I invite any of you who would like to keep in touch, to speak to me before I leave on Friday and I will be happy to give you my new phone and e-mail co-ordinates.

My very best wishes for the future go out to each and every one of you.

Yours sincerely,

Jason Hurley

BUSINESS PROPOSAL LETTERS

A business-to-business "proposal letter" is one that a company uses to make or submit a proposal or proposition to another company or organization.

The following pages contain real-life templates of business-to-business project letters.

Business Proposal Letters

Proposal – Business Service Partnership (pg. 208)
Proposal – Academic Partnership (pg. 209)
Proposal – Special Event (pg. 210)

To see some additional Business Proposal Letters go to page 119.

Note On Template Size

Please note that the letter templates on the following pages have been reduced in size slightly from what I consider ideal so that they could fit onto single pages of this guide. Because of this, the top and bottom margins are wider than what is recommended for a standard business letter (see pg 45). In addition, a point size of 11 has been used rather than the ideal size of 12 points.

Proposal: (business service partnership)

(print Professional Proposal Letter on corporate or personal letterhead)

Vijay Gupta, MD
725 Fairweather Drive
Burr Ridge, IL 60525

May 20, 20xx

Rhonda Trainer, MD
Head, Surgical Services
Southland Medical Clinic
755 Southland Clinic Boulevard
Venice, FL 34283

Dear Dr. Trainer:

I am currently an assistant professor at Wambaugh University Medical Center practicing general dermatology with a focus on contact dermatitis and patch testing. I will soon be relocating to Southwest Florida and am seeking an opportunity to provide comprehensive patch testing services to Floridians. As a highly respected tertiary care institution, I believe that Southland Clinic would be the ideal organization to service this niche and provide this vital service to the local community.

I completed my dermatology residency at University of Miami in 20XX and have been practicing general dermatology, with a focus on ethnic skin, hair disorders, occupational and contact dermatitis at Wambaugh University Medical Center for the past seven years and at Pineview VA hospital for the past five years; both located in the Cleveland, Ohio area. I am currently the director of our Contact Dermatitis Clinic and provide patch testing for more than 100 allergens. As you probably know, very few physicians in Southwest Florida provide this valuable service to the community. I therefore believe that comprehensive patch testing has the potential for significant growth in the Southwest Florida area.

I have attached a copy of my curriculum vitae for your review. If you have any questions or would like to set up a meeting I can be reached at xxx-xxx-xxxx.

I thank you in advance for your consideration and I am looking forward to an opportunity to discuss with you the potential for patch testing at the Southland Clinic.

Sincerely,

Vijay Gupta, MD
Assistant Professor of Medicine
Division of Dermatology

Attach:

Proposal: (academic partnership)

(print Institutional Proposal Letter on corporate letterhead paper)

April 12, 20xx

Dr. Andrew Randall
Director of Education Programs
Constitution College
75 Green Mountain Street
Concord, NH 03300

Dear Dr. Randall:

I would like to thank you for your recent letter confirming your interest in developing a mutually beneficial relationship between our two institutions. My appreciation goes out as well to President Johnson for his letter dated April 15, 20XX, in which he graciously accepted our invitation to participate with us as a distinguished research partner.

As I indicated in my letter to President Johnson, our institution is currently embarking on an ambitious plan to strengthen its degree programs and expand its research activities with the aim of becoming one of the top academic and research institutions in the world. Central to that program's success is our quest to develop joint research initiatives in various scientific fields with selected premier world institutions such as yours. We are therefore honored that we will be able to work as colleagues with your institution's distinguished leaders and outstanding faculty members to realize the objectives of our ambitious strategic plan.

Following receipt of President Johnson's letter of interest, I requested the appropriate departments here to develop a draft proposed framework agreement that would identify the areas of interest that our mutual cooperation might encompass. Once such areas of common interest are agreed upon by both parties, I would look forward to welcoming you and other officers of your institution to formally sign the Cooperation Agreement in the near future.

Accordingly, with your permission, I have taken the liberty of drafting the enclosed sample agreement for your review. You will notice that the draft Cooperation Agreement is titled "service contract" agreement. That is the standard terminology that we use for all of our cooperation agreements with distinguished institutions. Such a title is necessary to meet various administrative and legal requirements that govern our budgetary process.

I hope that the proposed areas of cooperation that we have put forward are acceptable to you. I look forward to receiving your views and comments in the near future.

Thank you again for your support and cooperation.

Sincerely,

Jeffrey Hutchinson
Director, Education Programs

Encl:

Proposal: (special event)

(print Business Proposal Letter on corporate letterhead paper)

December 15, 20xx

Mr. Nadim Dalwal
English Language Coordinator
Dar Al-Jandal School, Riyadh

Dear Mr. Dalwal:

Subject: Proposal To Hold An ELT Book Fair At Your School

Dar Al Jarad Publishing and Distribution House is pleased to invite your school to host an English Language Teaching (ELT) book fair.

We at Dar Al Jarad believe it is essential that we work directly with schools in Riyadh in order to enhance English literacy among students. We have chosen to approach your school to host one of these events because we are aware of your high educational standards and your interest in improving English literacy at your school.

Objectives:
Our objectives for holding the book fair at your school are as follows:
- To empower both teachers and students with our valuable ELT educational resources which include: readers, textbooks, support materials, and exam books.
- To introduce the students and the teachers to new ELT resources that are available in the market and how these resources can enhance literacy in the classroom.
- To familiarize parents with new ELT materials and the selection process that Curricular Coordinators go through when developing an English program.

Benefits:
Direct benefits that will come from hosting a book fair will be:
- The school will receive valuable publicity which will result in increased student enrolment.
- 15% of the proceeds from each title sold will go toward supporting the school's English program.
- The school staff and administration will work closely with the ELT distributor which will enhance cooperation between the school and Dar Al Jarad.

Arrangements:
- Your school will choose an appropriate date and duration for the event and advise our company of such.
- The school will advertise and promote the event to students, teachers and parents through its own channels.
- We are willing to assist in the advertising campaign by designing and printing brochures for the school to hand out to the students.
- The school will designate an appropriate location for the event, which will then be inspected by our staff to determine how many titles can be accommodated.
- Dar Al Jarad will supply and assemble all shelving at the designated location.
- During the event our staff will hand out free promotional materials.
- At the end of the event we will remove our products and leave behind free samples for use by the school.

Dar Al Jarad Publishing and Distribution looks forward to receiving a positive response from you on this proposal. We strongly believe that the educational benefits from such a function far outweigh any material considerations. If you have any questions about the above proposal please contact me at xxxxxxx.

We look forward to receiving your response in the near future.

Sincerely,

Reynata Darwish

PROJECT AND CONTRACT LETTERS

Business-to-business "project letters" and "contract letters" are used to transmit project and/or contract-related information to another company or organization. Typical project letters would include project status reports, proposal letters, and cost estimates.

The following pages contain real-life templates of some business-to-business project and contract letters.

Project and Contract Letters

To see some additional Project-related Letters go to page 119.

Note On Template Size

Please note that the letter templates on the following pages have been reduced in size slightly from what I consider ideal so that they could fit onto single pages of this guide. Because of this, the top and bottom margins are wider than what is recommended for a standard business letter (see pg 45). In addition, a point size of 11 has been used rather than the ideal size of 12 points.

Project: (letter of interest)

(print Letter of Interest for project participation on corporate letterhead)

November 18, 20xx

Mr. Raymond Fielding
President
Campus Renaissance Inc.
1850 Highridge Road
Columbus, Ohio 43201

Dear Raymond:

Mitchell-Maxwell and Timberline Properties are pleased to submit herewith our letter of interest to participate in your "campus neighborhood redevelopment project".

Since being invited to address this exciting opportunity, our team members have collaborated to produce a preliminary plan that we believe will energize the neighborhood, strengthen the University community, and produce long-term benefits for the entire City of Columbus.

As you know, we are a team of professionals with a proven track record in this region that has the ability to successfully transform our plan into reality. Our team is comprised of members who have worked together on numerous successful projects. They have been assembled for this project because of the enormous trust and confidence they have in one another. You can be assured that the lead partners in our group will manage the project closely and carefully; and accountability for results will never be delegated.

In the weeks ahead, we look forward to receiving comments from Campus Renaissance and the community at large about our preliminary proposal during the public consultation process. We understand that right now the plan is clearly a 'work in progress' which can only be improved by input from the various stakeholders who care the most about the area in question. We therefore look forward to using their input to develop a comprehensive integrated final development plan.

Thank you for giving us the opportunity to participate in this exciting project.

Sincerely,

_____   _____
Mary Louise Lasser   Roy Gooding
Timberline Properties   Mitchell-Maxwell

Project: (letter of credit)

(print project Letter of Credit on bank letterhead paper)

LETTER OF CREDIT

May 15, 20xx

City of Wentworth
Public Works Department
Construction and Engineering Branch
2450 Longfellow Road
Wentworth, OR, 97212

To Whom It May Concern:

Re: Letter of Credit - Hilton Construction Inc.: Project W-075-290 - Repave Access Roads

Please be advised that we have placed a hold on the line of credit of Hilton Construction Inc. in the amount of $525,000 for the benefit of the City of Wentworth for the work related to the above-noted public improvement project.

This hold is effective May 15, 20xx and will remain in effect until the work is completed and approved by the City of Wentworth.

West Coast Bank will secure said funds as a guarantee to the City of Wentworth for completion of the named public improvements in accordance with City permits.

Funds guaranteed by said line of credit will only be restored to Hilton Construction Inc. after West Coast Bank has received written confirmation from the Director of Construction and Engineering Services of the City of Wentworth that said improvements have been satisfactorily completed in accordance with the approved construction permit.

West Coast Bank agrees to disperse funds from the line of credit to the City of Wentworth upon written demand of the Director of Construction and Engineering Services, accompanied by the statement that conditions of the construction permit have been violated.

This is an irrevocable commitment of funds which is not subject to recall by Hilton Construction Inc.

Sincerely,

_____
John Livingstone
Corporate Credit Department

We Concur with this agreement:

_____
Fred Jackson
President

Contract: (expedite payment request)

(print Contract Letters on corporate letterhead paper)

June 12, 20xx

Mr. Randall McNeill
Director, Contract Administration
Illinois Project Consortium
25535 North Riverwoods Boulevard
90 North West, Mettawa
Illinois 60045

Dear Mr. McNeill:

Re: Request To Expedite Payment - Contract PLC-09-17542

Due to circumstances beyond our control, we have been unable to complete the final delivery phase of the exterior wharf retaining wall under the above-noted contract. All work has been completed except for the installation of the tie-down anchors which have not yet been received from the manufacturer. These are expected to arrive within four weeks and we plan to install them as soon as we receive them.

In the meantime, we are experiencing a serious cash flow problem which is affecting our ability to complete a number of our other contracts; including the access road extension project (PLC-10-21743). As you know, any delay in completion of the access road will have a negative impact on a number of other Phase 2 contracts.

We therefore request that you immediately release payment for the above-noted wharf retaining wall contract, subject to a 10% holdback to be payable on completion of the tie-down anchors. That arrangement will protect you while at the same time relieving the problems caused by our current cash flow difficulties.

Accordingly, please find attached an invoice for the final progress payment of $67,575 for contract PLC-09-17542.

If you have any questions at all please contact me immediately at 312-752-3479.

On behalf of our entire company I thank you in advance for your kind cooperation.

Sincerely,

Charles Strathem
Construction Contracts Manager

Attach:

Contract: (provide background information)

(print Contract Letters on corporate letterhead paper)

September 14, 20xx

Vincent Carvillo
Vice President
Contrext Construction Ltd.
HSBR Towers, Suite A-1520
18 Canada Square
London E14 5HQ

Dear Mr. Carvillo:

This is further to Veronica Brabham's letter to you dated August 20, 20xx which requested that you supply us with additional information on Contrext Construction's accounting system and related methodologies.

Efforts to-date to obtain the requested information have been unsuccessful. Therefore, you are hereby notified that you must submit the information mentioned above directly to this office by September 30, 20xx. Please be further advised that no more requests for time extensions will be considered.

As you are aware, this office is making a concerted effort to bring this matter to a close. For that to happen it is important that you submit the supporting documentation requested in Ms. Brabham's August 20th letter. Upon receipt of that information, our Director, Contracts Accounting will immediately review it, after which this office will notify you of the findings. If you do not respond by the above-noted deadline, this office will be forced to proceed with an alternative course of action.

It is imperative that you make every effort to submit the requested information by the specified due date. Otherwise, we will not be able to process your current outstanding invoices.

If you have any questions or concerns please contact the undersigned immediately: by phone at (420) 862-3992; by email at accounts@binghamgroup.com; or by fax at (420) 862-5304.

Thank you in advance for your kind cooperation.

Sincerely,

Catherine Shorter
Head, Accounts Management

Contract: (notice of audit)

(print Contract Letters on corporate letterhead paper)

May 25, 20xx

Mr. Dominic Rafael
President and CEO
Jenson Structures Inc.
505 Granville Street, 12th Floor
Vancouver, British Columbia
Canada V6C 2R6

Dear Mr. Rafael:

Re: Notice of Intent To Conduct An Audit

Further to our recent phone conversation, this is to formally advise you that the Olympic Construction Committee has decided to request an audit of the accounting practices of Jenson Structures Inc. The audit will commence immediately and will be performed on behalf of the OCC by Taylor & Hanson Auditing Services Inc. of Vancouver.

As you know, this audit was prompted by some serious invoice/work order discrepancies that were noted during a number of our transaction-sampling mini-audits that were conducted over the past six months. When briefed on the results of these mini-audits, the OCC decided that an immediate audit of Jenson's accounting practices and procedures with respect to invoicing was warranted.

The audit will be conducted in full accordance with the OCC's contract administration and control policy which is an addendum to all of our construction contracts. Among other things, that policy states that "…all outstanding invoices submitted by the company being audited will be held in abeyance until such time as the results of the audit are known." Also in accordance with the policy, "… depending on the results of the audit, it will be at the Committee's sole discretion to determine when, and to what degree, any payments will be made to cover any outstanding invoices."

We look forward to your complete cooperation with the auditors so that the audit can be conducted quickly and concluded as soon as possible.

If you have any questions about the audit process please feel free to contact the Project Senior Auditor, Janice Gonzalez, at 604-459-4115.

Sincerely,

Gordon Cranston
Chairman, OCC Accountability Committee

Contract: (cancellation notice)

(print Letter of Contract Termination on personal or business stationery)

4500 Gables Road
Suite 1027
Miami, FL 33170

December 12, 20xx

Vanessa Redden
Head, Small Publisher Services
Publish Me Now Inc.
1200 NW 25th St.
Suite 1225
Miami, FL 33172

Dear Ms. Redden:

Re: How-To Publications Inc. - Notice of Contract Cancellation

Please regard this as my official written notice to terminate all contractual arrangements that I have with your company regarding publication of the works of How-To Publications Inc., of which I am the President and Owner. This termination is to take full effect December 31, 20xx.

As you will remember, when I signed up with PMN in early June, I did have my doubts and reservations about your service, but based on your assurances I decided to give your company a six-month trial run. With that trial period about to expire at the end of this month please regard this as the two weeks advance notice of cancellation, as required in the contract.

Based on my experience during the trial period it appears that many of my initial reservations were well-founded. In particular, I was very disappointed by your lack of a strong distribution network, which forced me to have to find and develop a network of book retailers and distributors on my own. In addition, your 100% refund policy coupled with your high discount rates and long payment delays seem almost punitive and make it difficult for a small publisher like me to make a decent return.

For your information, I have been able to find another service that offers much more favorable terms, and I will be working with that company beginning early next year.

Accordingly, would you please have your staff take the necessary action to remove all of my How-To Publications from your network by December 31, 20xx.

Sincerely,

Margaret Frankel

MARKETING AND PROMOTION LETTERS

A business-to-business or business-to-customer "marketing and/or promotion letter" is one that a company uses to make industry announcements or to promote its products or services throughout the industry marketplace in which it operates. Typical promotion letters would include new product and service announcements.

The following pages contain some real-life templates of business-to-business promotion letters.

Marketing and Promotion Letters

Marketing and Promotion – Promote Small Business (pg. 220)
Marketing and Promotion – Promote New Referral Program (pg. 221)
Marketing and Promotion – Announce New Program (pg. 222)

To see some other Marketing and Promotion Letters go to pages 109 and 179.

Note On Template Size

Please note that the letter templates on the following pages have been reduced in size slightly from what I consider ideal so that they could fit onto single pages of this guide. Because of this, the top and bottom margins are wider than what is recommended for a standard business letter (see pg 45). In addition, a point size of 11 has been used rather than the ideal size of 12 points.

Marketing and Promotion: (promote small business)

(print Business Promotion Letter on business letterhead paper)

March 15, 20xx

[client address line 1]
[client address line 2]
[client address line 3]
[client address line 4]

Dear [Name of Client]:

What if I told you that I can simplify your life AND save you money?

My name is Walter Dudinsky and I am a Certified Public Accountant (CPA) practicing in the San Francisco area. I have more than 25 years of experience helping my clients navigate the ever changing and increasingly complex taxation requirements, as well as acting as their buffer from the IRS.

Here is what I believe my CPA practice can do for you:

- Assess your current tax situation (business and/or personal) and find ways to optimize your taxation profile that will save you time, trouble and money.

- Act as your shield, buffer, and interpreter in dealings with the IRS.

- Advise you and help you deal with any outstanding and/or unresolved tax issues.

- Advise you on a wide range of topics from accounting matters, to taxes, to estate planning.

- Work in partnership with you to ensure that you and/or your business are always in front of the latest IRS tax requirement developments.

I know that you might be naturally reluctant to change your current accounting service, even if you are unhappy with it, just because it might seem like such a hassle. So, in order to get your serious consideration, I have decided that I will show you that I am serious about becoming your new CPA by offering you the following benefits with no strings attached:

- **One hour of free consultation** to review any and all taxation issues that you would like to discuss.

- **A free subscription** to my quarterly Individual and Business Tax Tips newsletter.

In addition, should you decide to transfer your accounting business to my practice, I will offer you complete transparency during the transition process.

Whether you have unresolved tax issues, or if you are current and just want a second opinion, please don't hesitate to call my office right away (626-685-4575) to set up **your free consultation** appointment.

Yours sincerely,

Walter Dudinsky, CPA

Marketing and Promotion: (new referral program)

(print Marketing Promotion Letter on business letterhead paper)

February 20, 20xx

[client address line 1]
[client address line 2]
[client address line 3]
[client address line 4]

Dear [Client Name]:

Try My New Easy Money Customer Referral Program!

As you know, I take a tremendous amount of pride in the level of service and commitment I give to each and every one of my clients. I have developed many close relationships in my role as a tax advisor and believe I possess the expertise and experience that distinguishes me from my peers.

I am now ready to take my practice to the next level and, frankly, I need your help. I have tried many marketing strategies over the years but have found that, without question, the most successful way of acquiring a new client is through a direct referral from an existing, satisfied client, which I believe you to be.
Now before you get nervous that I'm going to ask you for 10 names and phone numbers, let me put you at ease! I get very uncomfortable when my friends and business associates ask me for referrals. I also get a little put off when a stranger cold-calls me out of the blue and tells me that so-and-so gave him my name and he wants to meet with me and discuss the wonders of his product or service. Some people are fine with that approach but I think most folks would admit it is a little unsettling. Consequently, I have developed a system that will allow you to refer someone to me without any anxiety.

Along with this letter, I've included business referral cards that you can use to introduce me to your friends, family, and business associates. These referral cards were designed to take the "referral burden" off of your shoulders. Simply hand them out (Along with a gushing verbal endorsement of me, of course!) and you're done. The postcard will direct the person to my website where they can read my bio, view a video about what I do, and decide on their own whether to schedule an appointment with me. It will also tell them how they can get a free copy of my valuable handbook "How To Deal With the IRS".

Here's the best part – I won't ask you for the name of anyone you refer. In fact, I would prefer that you not offer me their name. If your referral contacts me directly from the website, that's terrific. I'll give them the same personal service I've given you. If, for whatever reason, they don't feel a meeting is warranted, I'll never know. No matter how someone contacts me, when they do, the very first thing I will ask them is how they got my information. If they give your name I will immediately send you the $10 finder fee. If they then decide to become a paying client I will send you the additional $25 sign-up fee!

I am very excited to be offering you an opportunity to be a participant in this new referral system. I suggest that when you have the time you pay a brief visit to my website (www.dougwarden-taxservices.com) to see what your referrals will be seeing. Please let me know if you need additional postcards.

I want you to know that I am sending you this letter because I consider you an ideal client. I want to continue to work with people like you who are friendly, positive and appreciative. I would therefore ask you to please keep that in mind whenever you are considering a referral.

Sincerely,

Doug Warden

Encl.

Marketing and Promotion: (announce new program)

(print Business Promotion Letter on corporate letterhead paper)

September 30, 20xx

Dealer address – Line 1
Dealer address – Line 2
Dealer address – Line 3
Dealer address – Line 4

Dear [Dealer Name]:

This Program Is Guaranteed To Grow Your Business!

I am very excited to announce to you my new FREE 90-Day Home Warranty Program! This limited-time offer is being made exclusively to my long-time agents and it is limited to the first 100 paid inspections performed.

This valuable home warranty program is being underwritten by Home Warranty Services of America a highly dependable, licensed and bonded home warranty underwriter in South Carolina.
To qualify to offer this **FREE 90-Day Home Warranty Program** to your customers, all you need to do is register as a participant using the enclosed Program Registration Form. We will contact you with your Program Certificate Number within a few days of receiving your registration form. Once you have that number you can schedule and conduct your customer home inspections under the program.

It is important to note that when your inspection is complete you must have the customer pay in-full at the time of the inspection. (Because of the way the **FREE 90-Day-HomeWarranty Program** is structured I cannot defer payment until closing; so all fees are due immediately upon completion of the inspection.)

I hope you will take advantage of this limited-quantity **FREE 90-Day Home Warranty Program** offer and pass it along to your customers as a valuable incentive. Once you are a registered participant you may offer this program to your customers until midnight December 31, 20xx.

Enclosed is a sample term-coverage contract for your information. If you have any questions, please contact me at xxx-xxx-xxxx.

Yours sincerely,

Hector Gomez

Enclosures

RECOMMENDATION LETTERS

Business-to-business recommendation letters are normally used by a business to positively recommend its staff or former employees to another business or organization.

Recommendation Letters

To see some other business-related Recommendation Letters go to pages 129 and 187.

Note On Template Size

Please note that the letter templates on the following pages have been reduced in size slightly from what I consider ideal so that they could fit onto single pages of this guide. Because of this, the top and bottom margins are wider than what is recommended for a standard business letter (see pg 45). In addition, a point size of 11 has been used rather than the ideal size of 12 points.

Recommendation: (business colleague)

(print Reference Letter on company letterhead paper)

850 Harcourt Road
Dublin 2
Ireland

April 20, 20xx

Addressee Line 1
Addressee Line 2
Addressee Line 3
Addressee Line 4

Dear Sir/Madam:

Subject: Letter of Reference – Winston Prince

I have known Winston Prince since September 20xx when we met during the Orientation Programme as we began our careers at Bromberg L.P.

As a colleague, I quickly developed a sense of respect and admiration for Winston. Even in those early days, it was evident to me that he was a bright, thoughtful, and articulate person. I could also see that he was very passionate about whatever he did or believed, with a natural ability to engage others.

Winston and I both started our careers in analytics. His thirst for knowledge meant that he was constantly learning about different markets. Soon we were all turning to him for help with client questions. Our careers followed similar paths into Sales, where Winston's passion and work ethic quickly earned him the recognition and respect of management. He was soon promoted to manage the North of England account.

Working with Winston on a number of projects and sales teams I could see that he was a highly focused, energetic and driven professional. He consistently took on challenging roles and then performed over and above what was expected of him. It was the norm for him to over-deliver.

Winston is a natural leader and doesn't hesitate to assume a leadership role. Due to frequent requests from his peers for help, he took it upon himself to organise weekly clinics on Excel and Fixed Income software, in which he answered his colleague's questions. With his quick intellect and natural sense of humour, Winston added a lot of charm and wit to his seminars and workshops. In fact, he is one of the rare few who can keep an audience interested in subjects as dry as "bond math swap valuation".

I always admired Winston's sense of purpose and discipline, when during our train journeys back to London he would find time to run through his CFA flash cards. He has an amazing ability to focus and compartmentalize, and he never loses sight of his goals.

I believe that Winston's departure was a great loss to our sales team and to the company as a whole.

Based on my experience working with Winston Prince, I can strongly recommend him as a candidate for any business program to which he might apply. I am confident he would make an invaluable contribution to that institution. If you have any further questions please don't hesitate to contact me at + 44 xx xxxx xxx xxx.

Sincerely,

Tom Mendes
Senior Marketing Associate
Bromberg L.P.

Recommendation: (business associate)

(print Recommendation Letter on personal letterhead paper)

215 North Street
St Andrews, KY16 9AJ

December 20, 20xx

Postgraduate Admissions Office
University of Aberdeen
King's College
Aberdeen, AB24 3FX

Dear Admissions Director:

I have known and worked with Miss Samantha Wu for almost five years and based on that I am delighted to recommend her for your MBA programme.

I am currently an associate professor at St. Andrews University in the United Kingdom. For the past 20 months, I have had the pleasure of working with Samantha on the Mustard Seed Project, an educational project for school children in remote areas of South East Asia and China. As her project partner, I have seen Samantha demonstrate outstanding leadership in motivating others to participate in the project as well as through her efforts in initiating and operating the project. Below I share my assessments of some of Samantha's key attributes.

I first met Samantha in Yunnan Province of China in 20xx, while we were working on a documentary film project. We discovered that we both cared deeply about human rights matters and discussed many educational issues. In 20xx, Samantha sent me a proposal to help her set up a project to assist school children in remote areas have better access to educational resources and change the way they see the outside world. She believed that many school children in remote areas of South East Asia and China ran away from home to the outside world with a dream of escaping from poverty but instead ended up involved in prostitution or drug dealing. The plan was to encourage travelling backpackers to share their real-life knowledge of the world outside with school children in those remote areas while the backpackers themselves could benefit from opportunities to explore the local cultures. Samantha's ideas and passion convinced me, and I was the first person to get involved in the project and later became her primary project partner. Later on, other post graduate students also joined the project.

Compared with the leaders and participants of other non-profit organizations or projects in which I have participated, such as the Irish Agriculture Farmers project and the Xuannan Primary School Volunteer project (China), Samantha stands out in a number of ways.

1. **Persistency in initiating the project**
   Over a three year period Samantha actively participated in various non-profit organizations so that she could learn from their operations. During the Mustard Seed Project initiation, many of us thought the project scope was too small. In response, Samantha called several meetings to discuss the scope, where she shared her experiences in similar small non-profit projects. After a few follow-up emails, the team united and reached a shared goal that: in three years we would have volunteers teaching programs in three schools. She then led us through the detailed planning tasks for achieving that goal. Step by step, she taught us to pursue our vision in a realistic way. Samantha also showed respect for the ambitious ideas of team members by placing our previous big plans in different project phases. Her persistence in building the team was the foundation that allowed us to move forward.

2. **Discipline to manage the project**
   Compared with other community projects in which I have been involved, Samantha operates the Mustard Seed Project team very efficiently and keeps us on track at all times. She sends out regular email reminders to advise us of our progress and she insists on meetings of the core team once every two weeks to discuss the issues and current tasks, even when she is on business trips. She also sends out decision records and

follow-up assignments after each meeting. In a small scope non-profit project where everyone has only limited time to devote, her management skills keep the progress of the project on schedule.

3. **Flexibility to communicate internal and external**

   Samantha demonstrates superior communication skills while dealing with people from a variety of backgrounds including; project team members (mostly post-graduate students), local partners who are local small businessmen, and volunteer backpackers. As the project leader, she listens to and respects our opinions and always makes sure we fully understand the reason behind her decisions and are comfortable with them. When building partnerships with local communities for the Mustard Seed Project, she always first listens to the opinions of the locals about educational issues facing school children, and only after that does she explain the design of our courses and the mission of our project. She sees the project from the perspectives of both the project team and the local community. She knows how to successfully earn the trust of local community groups first. When dealing with project volunteers, Samantha always addresses the benefits from both the local school children's angle and also from the perspectives of volunteers. She emphasizes the unique local cultures and environments that will enrich the volunteers' travel experience.

As the founder and the leader of the Mustard Seed Project, Samantha has had a major impact. In the past 20 months she has led us to many achievements including: completing the teaching materials, building connections with local communities, completion of one volunteer teaching session in Pang Numtrang School in Thailand, and building a partnership with a local businessman there to advertise our project in his hostel. However, I believe her impact on this project goes beyond just making it happen or operating it. Samantha's passionate but down-to-earth personality has influenced us not to just dream about changing, but also to find, plan, and execute the changes. This is one of the main strengths she offers the non-profit world -- a pragmatic approach backed up by concrete and proven methods.

Overall, I think Samantha Wu is a person with big dreams and serious plans who has the ability to achieve them. I believe that by studying at your institution, she will get closer to her dream of making an impact on the world.

Based on the foregoing, without reservation, I am pleased to highly recommend Samantha Wu for acceptance into your programme. If you have any questions, please do not hesitate to contact me.

Sincerely,

Jill Wong
St. Andrews University, UK
School of Social Anthropology

Recommendation: (employee travel visa)

(print corporate Recommendation Letter on corporate letterhead)

April 12, 20xx

Canadian Visa Office
400 Water Street
Los Angeles, CA 91101

Dear Visa Officer:

I am writing this recommendation letter on behalf of Mr. Sheldon Wong, our Senior Developer and Program Manager. Mr. Wong is planning to attend the Canadian Institute's Annual Forum on Anti-Money Laundering in Toronto from April 28 to April 29 as a representative of CCC (California Collections Services, Inc.). Accordingly, CCS assumes all financial responsibility for any debts that may be incurred by Mr. Wong during his brief stay in Canada.

CCS is currently helping a growing number of top lenders that offer credit card, real estate, student, and instalment loan products, to manage their charged-off, delinquent, and pre-delinquent portfolio operations. Our potential clients include BMO (Bank of Montreal) in Canada. The information and contacts acquired by Mr. Wong in this meeting will help our company build an improved collections system that will better protect our client organizations from fraud as well as other financial risks such as money laundering.

We are actively sponsoring Mr. Wong's U.S. green card application which will allow him to work permanently in the United States. We look forward to his continued contribution in building a better risk management system for CCS.

I thank you in advance for your cooperation and assistance in the timely processing of Mr. Wong's visa application so that he may attend the above-mentioned forum on our behalf.

Should you have any questions, please do not hesitate to contact me by e-mail at: xxxxxxxxxx, or you can call me directly at xxx-xxx-xxxx.

Very sincerely,

Leonard Ranford
CEO, California Collection Services, Inc.

FINANCIAL HARDSHIP LETTERS

Business-to-business Financial Hardship Letters are typically sent by a business to a bank, financial services company, or government agency, seeking some type of financial relief.

Financial Hardship Letters

Financial Hardship – Consolidate and Restructure Debt (pg. 230)
Financial Hardship – Provide Background Information (pg. 231)
Financial Hardship – Request For Short Sale (pg. 232)

The previous edition of this Kit did not contain any financial hardship letters.

Note On Template Size

Please note that the letter templates on the following pages have been reduced in size slightly from what I consider ideal so that they could fit onto single pages of this guide. Because of this, the top and bottom margins are wider than what is recommended for a standard business letter (see pg 45). In addition, a point size of 11 has been used rather than the ideal size of 12 points.

Financial Hardship: (consolidate/restructure debt)

(print Financial Hardship Letter on company letterhead paper)

April 20, 20xx

Mr. Donald Gustafson
Manager, Business Credit Services
Great Lakes Financial Services Inc.
3590 Drayton Avenue, Suite 750
Santa Monica, CA 95040

Dear Mr. Gustafson:

Re: Request For Debt Consolidation and Restructuring – Marbank Enterprises Inc.

Marbank Enterprises Inc. has been dealing with your company since our founding, 18 years ago. The purpose of this letter is to request your assistance in helping us remain operational during a period of temporary financial hardship.

For almost two decades we have been a successful importer and wholesaler of electronic products from Asia. Unfortunately, in recent months we have started to suffer from the effects of the widespread "mini-recession" that struck the US economy last year. The primary reason for our cash flow problems is that sales of electronic products to end-consumers declined by more than 30% over a few months, leaving us with excess unsold inventory for which we have already paid. We are convinced this is a temporary situation. Industry experts and economic indexes are indicating that we should be able to move this excess inventory within a few months.

We are therefore requesting two things from your company that will give us the short-term flexibility relief that we need to keep operating profitably in the near term:

1. We would like an extension to our existing line of credit from $500K to $1 million. This would give us the flexibility we need to deal with this cash flow deficit over the next 6 to 12 months without negative impacts on any of our ongoing profitable operations.

2. We would like to consolidate our two main outstanding business credit card account balances (total of $425K) and pay them off using the extended $1 million line of credit. This would allow us to then open one of your new Business Prime accounts at a much lower interest rate than the 6.95% that we currently pay. In essence, we would simply be transferring our current debt from a higher interest account to one with a much more manageable interest rate.

To help you assess our financial situation, I have attached a set of Marbank's financial statements from last operating year, and a sales forecast to the end of the current business year. You will notice that our current paid-up inventory is valued at $1.2 million. We expect to be able to sell at least 50% of this over the next six months.

On behalf of our management team and Marbank's 45 employees, I very much appreciate your consideration in this matter and look forward to hearing from you in the near future. If you have any questions, please don't hesitate to contact me at 831-529-5477.

Yours sincerely,

David Smeltzer
Chief Operating Officer

attach: Marbank Enterprises Inc. - Financial Statements - 20xx
          Marbank sales and cashflow projections – current year

Financial Hardship: (provide background information)

(print personal/business Financial Hardship Letter on personal stationery)

1575 California St.
Denver, CO 80202

February 29, 20xx

Mr. Rodney Naulter
Senior Vice-President
Vista Peaks Estates
735 Londoner Road
Denver, CO 80255

Dear Mr. Naulter:

This is further to your recent request for background on my current business and personal financial situation.

I spent more than 12 years building up my financial services and mortgage-banking company from scratch into a successful going concern. During that period I was so committed to that family business that almost all retained annual earnings were channelled right back into the business. That reinvestment strategy worked well in good times but when we ran into cash flow problems there were no ready cash reserves to draw from.

At its peak, the company had 132 employees in five offices situated across the USA. Ongoing operating costs ranged as high as $600,000 per month as they covered employee salaries, healthcare benefits, payroll taxes, office leasing costs, supplier and vendor payments, etc. Tragically, all of this came crashing down quite suddenly in early 20xx as my company became one more casualty of the nationwide and global collapse of the financial and credit markets. As cash flow quickly dried up, we were forced to lay-off all of our employees and shut down operations in a matter of weeks. Due to that widespread market crisis, our primary income source, loan originations - stopped coming in almost overnight.

I did everything within my power to keep the company afloat. We had to borrow funds from private lenders and establish emergency lines of credit against the equity in our properties. All of our cash reserves and equity at the time went directly into covering monthly overheads as we tried to weather the storm. Sadly, none of these measures were enough, and the company was forced to cease operations in December 20xx. Since I had given personal guarantees to Wall Street credit institutions, I was forced to seek credit protection and consequently filed for bankruptcy. It is such a cruel irony that, as a long-time lender and advocate that one should always strive hard to protect their credit, I am now the one with credit difficulties.

My wife Sharon who has been the primary caregiver to our three children is back to work in her profession as an interior designer and decorating specialist. I have successfully rekindled my investor relationships and am fully involved in assisting my clients to acquire, renovate and resell their properties. To-date, we have completed more than 17 projects and our order lists continues to grow and expand into the next few years.

My wife and I have carefully reviewed our financial situation and have concluded that it would be prudent (at least for the next two years) to rent and gradually rebuild our savings towards a large down payment for the purchase of a home in which to live and operate our new business in the future. In the meantime, we want our three children (ages 7, 10, and 13) to continue to feel secure living in a home that has the spacious feeling, natural light and warmth like the home you are offering for rent. It is in the same neighborhood in which they have lived since they were toddlers. We would be deeply grateful for your assistance in allowing this to happen.

We look forward to a positive response and thank you in advance for your kind consideration.

Sincerely,

Brendan H. Sifton

Financial Hardship: (request for short sale)

(print Financial Hardship Letter on personal or business stationery)

450 Craighurst Dr.
Denver, CO 80260

June 20, 20xx

Mr. Walter Prentiss
Vice President, Business Credit
Morgan-Bentley Savings and Trust
2575 Sherman Ave.
Denver, CO 80261

Dear Mr. Prentiss:

Re: Request For Short Sale - 450 Craighurst Drive., Denver CO

I am writing this hardship letter to you as advised by Mary Bronson, Manager, at your Mountain Branch.

I am the owner and operator of Flite Aviation Maintenance Services Inc.. In January of this year I was forced to lay off my 27 employees and temporarily shut down the business due to difficult economic times in the aviation business. As you are no doubt aware, over the past 18 months there has been a general downturn in the aviation industry worldwide caused by high oil and fuel prices. When the airlines cut back their flight operations it had a direct impact on my business since there are fewer airplanes to service and maintain.

Although most of the experts agree that this is a temporary situation, it has already impacted me and my family; and we are in imminent danger of defaulting on our home mortgage. Ever since the temporary shut-down of the company we have been struggling to make ends meet. We have already gone through most of our savings and our only source of income, my wife Angela's annual salary of $38K as a researcher is barely enough to support our three children, and cannot cover our total family living costs including mortgage payments. Consequently, for the past six months we have had no other choice but to cover the monthly mortgage payments for the above-noted address out of our family savings. Unfortunately, after two more payments those savings will be completely gone. To add insult to injury, we recently learned that our house is now worth far less than it was when we purchased it three years ago, due to the general downturn in the real estate market across the country. Finally, our 7-year old daughter Grace was diagnosed this January with a form of cystic fibrosis. Although treatable, the total monthly cost of her medications is $575 which is not covered by insurance.

I am currently job hunting in the aviation field while we wait for my company business to pick up; but things don't look too promising given the current state of the industry. Even if I am lucky enough to somehow land a job in my field we wouldn't be able to cover all of our family's monthly expenses, especially with the added cost of my daughter's medicines. I have attached a monthly cash flow statement that clearly shows our monthly shortfall; as well as a letter from the specialist detailing our daughter's condition and the medications required.

My wife and I have carefully reviewed our financial situation with an accountant friend and have concluded that the only possible way our family can survive financially is to sell the house to eliminate the monthly mortgage payment of $1,785. We know of an acceptable three bedroom apartment that will become available for rent in three months at $895 per month where we could live comfortably until we get back on our feet financially.

In light of the above, I humbly and respectfully request that you allow us to execute a short sale of our house as soon as possible so that we may avoid mortgage foreclosure and financial ruin. I can be reached at 720-785-1545 if you have any questions or require additional information.

Very sincerely,

Frank Rasmussen

Attach: Monthly cash flow statement

CONDOLENCE AND SYMPATHY LETTERS

Business-to-business condolence and sympathy letters are typically sent from an officer of a business in situations where an employee or family member of an employee has passed away.

Condolence and Sympathy Letters

Condolence – To Brother of Deceased (pg. 234)
Sympathy – To Family of Deceased (pg. 235)
Sympathy - To Spouse of Deceased (pg. 236)

To see some other business-related Condolence Letters go to page 187.

Note On Template Size

Please note that the letter templates on the following pages have been reduced in size slightly from what I consider ideal so that they could fit onto single pages of this guide. Because of this, the top and bottom margins are wider than what is recommended for a standard business letter (see pg 45). In addition, a point size of 11 has been used rather than the ideal size of 12 points.

Condolence: (to brother of deceased)

(print business Letter of Condolence on business letterhead paper)

November 30, 20xx

Mr. Jim Hollingsworth
President and CEO
Penn Manufacturing Inc.
1260 North Washington Avenue
Scranton, Pennsylvania 18503

Dear Jim:

Please accept my sincere condolences for the sudden loss of your dear brother Ray last week. I can only imagine what a shock it must be to you and the PMI extended family. Indeed, it was only two weeks ago that Ray and I shared a table at the Mayor's annual fundraiser.

I know what a difficult loss this will be for you in particular. Not only will you miss your cherished brother but also a trusted business partner and advisor. I can only imagine the depth of the void that it will leave in your personal, family, and business lives.

As you know, Ray and I went back more than 20 years both as friends and business associates. Not only was he a great person to do business with, he was also an excellent golfing partner with whom I spent many memorable days on the links over the years. He had an amazing sense of humor and was a gifted storyteller. In business dealings Ray was always straightforward and as honest as the day is long. In short, your brother Ray was an exceptional friend, colleague and customer who will be deeply missed by all who knew him.

Would you please pass on my sincere condolences to all of the employees at Penn Manufacturing and let them know that we here at Allied Building Systems collectively mourn Ray's loss.

Sincere condolences,

Brad Fender

Sympathy: (to family of deceased)

(print Sympathy Letter to employee's family on corporate letterhead)

November 15, 20xx

Mrs. Edith Hampton
4575 Village Drive
Seattle, WA 98105-5032

Dear Mrs. Hampton:

I was deeply saddened to learn of Frank's death and I would like to express my sincere sympathy to you and your family on behalf of the senior management team here at Interconnect Corp. Your husband was highly respected by managers and employees alike throughout the entire company. He was regarded as a visionary leader by anyone who ever worked with him.

Frank's contributions to this company during his 27 years of dedicated and selfless service were many and varied. In the early years he was a major part of our initial expansion overseas, and a number of the offices he set up in Europe are still operating very successfully. In recent years Frank was a key player in our transformation to full digital technology, a move which catapulted us into a leadership position in the industry. Believe me, his contributions to this company will not be forgotten.

Please accept my heartfelt condolences at this difficult time and I ask you to please pass these sentiments on to your children. Your husband was a remarkable man in many ways. Knowing him personally as I did for many years, I am well aware of the difference he made in the lives of many people, both here in the company, and in his private life. He will be missed by many.

With sincere sympathy,

Charles T. Simpson
President and CEO

Sympathy: (to spouse of deceased)

(business-personal Letter of Sympathy should be hand-written)

895 Don Mills Road, Unit 2735
Toronto, ON
M3C 1T5

November 19, 20xx

Dear Sabrina,

Please let me express my deepest sympathies to you and the children. I was shocked and shattered when I heard about Bill's horrific accident. I can't even imagine what you have been going through for the past ten days.

As you know, Bill and I have been colleagues and friends for the past eight years. His tragic loss leaves a terrible void in our office. He was so well-liked and respected by everyone who came into contact with him, both colleagues and clients alike. He had tremendous people skills, and as such, was a role model in our company and the industry at large.

I trust that, when they are older, the children will be made aware of what an outstanding person Bill was in his professional life.

Sabrina, please feel free to contact me if I can help in any way while you go through this very difficult period. I will support you in any way that I can should you reach out to me.

Also, please tell the children how terribly devastated all of us are here at the company due to their Father's tragic passing.

Sincere sympathy,

Darlene Francis

OTHER BUSINESS LETTERS

These are miscellaneous business-to-business and business-to-customer letters that don't fall clearly into any of the previous major business letter categories.

The following pages contain a couple of real-life templates of uncategorized business-to-business and business-to-customer letters.

Other Business Letters

Other Letters – Customer Appreciation (pg. 238)
Other Letters – Proposal Cover Letter (pg. 239)

To see various uncategorized "other" business-related letters go to pages 129 and 187.

Note On Template Size

Please note that the letter templates on the following pages have been reduced in size slightly from what I consider ideal so that they could fit onto single pages of this guide. Because of this, the top and bottom margins are wider than what is recommended for a standard business letter (see pg 45). In addition, a point size of 11 has been used rather than the ideal size of 12 points.

Other Letters (customer appreciation)

(print Letter of Appreciation on business letterhead paper)

January 27, 20xx
"Special Customer" List
Customer Address Line 2
Customer Address Line 3
Customer Address Line 4

Dear [Customer First Name]:

Thank You For Your Business!

I am sending this letter to express my sincere appreciation to you for your continued patronage of our business. At European Interiors we are well aware that it is repeat customers like you who are largely responsible for 20xx being the best sales year in our 14 year history.

To say thank you in a more concrete way we would ask you to drop into the main store on Kirby Avenue before the end of February 20xx to pick up your free gift. We have managed to acquire a supply of hand crafted cedar boot racks for a few of our very special customers and we would like you to have one. In fact, we have one reserved in your name until the end of February, no strings attached.

In addition, we are also offering an exclusive financing package to only our best and most appreciated customers during that same period. Because you are included in that very exclusive group, we are offering you zero down payment, with zero financing charges for the entire first year of ownership of any furniture purchase you make valued over $1,000 during the month of February.

We are happy to have served you well in the past and we look forward to continuing to provide your home furnishing needs in the future.

When you come to the main store during February to pick up your gift please feel free to stop by my showroom office and say hello. I look forward to seeing you.

Yours with thanks,

Rachel Whittaker
General Manager

Other Letters (proposal cover letter)

September 12, 20xx

Richard Kendrick
General Manager
Valley Fitness, Inc.
17712 116th Way
Kent, WA 98802

Dear Mr. Kendrick:

Thank you for taking the time to talk with me last week. I know that your business office accounting has been a high priority problem for you. I am therefore pleased to propose a cost effective solution that I believe will minimize your in-house burden.

As I explained when we met, we are specialists in Accounting and Payroll services with more than 40 years of experience. We pride ourselves in providing our clients with a professional service, guaranteed accuracy, and the highest level of confidentiality.

The attached cost summary is based upon your current needs and can be adjusted as we customize your services.

I look forward to discussing this project with you in more detail in the near future.
Please contact me directly anytime you have additional questions or requests at 425-740-8478 (ext. 905).

Sincerely,

Veronica Hamilton
President
Applied Accounting Services

Attach:

WRITING BUSINESS REPORTS

Although this guide is focused on business letters, I thought that it would be a good thing to share some of my knowledge and experience on the subject of writing "business reports" as **a BONUS for anyone buying this book.**

After all, at some point just about everyone needs to know what a business report is (and is not), what one contains, and the basics of writing one.

Working as a consultant over the years in both the private and public sectors, I have written numerous business reports of many different types. I also had a formal refresher course on writing business reports when I went back to school to get my M.B.A. in the mid 1990s. It seemed that all we did there was to write one report after another!

After I completed my M.B.A. and went out on my own as a consultant, writing such reports became a major part of the way I earn my living for a number of years.

Accordingly, the following pages summarize some of the key lessons that I have learned over the years about writing every type of business report.

BUSINESS REPORT WRITING TIPS

People often cringe at the thought of writing a "business report". Granted, these may be a little more complicated than business letters, but if approached in the right way, writing a business report can be a straightforward and reasonably painless process.

There are a number of different generic types of business reports including: general business report, business plan, business proposal, marketing plan, strategic plan, business analysis, project report, project analysis, project proposal, project review, financial plan, financial analysis, and others.

Although the technical content and terminology will vary from report to report, depending on the subject and industry context, the actual "report writing process" will be essentially the same. Whether it's a short 10-pager, or a major 100-plus pager, that "process" will involve the same fundamental steps.

The Report Writing Process

The process that I have developed over the years for writing any type of business report is summarized in my "7 Key Steps" as follows:

7 Key Steps For Writing Better Business Reports

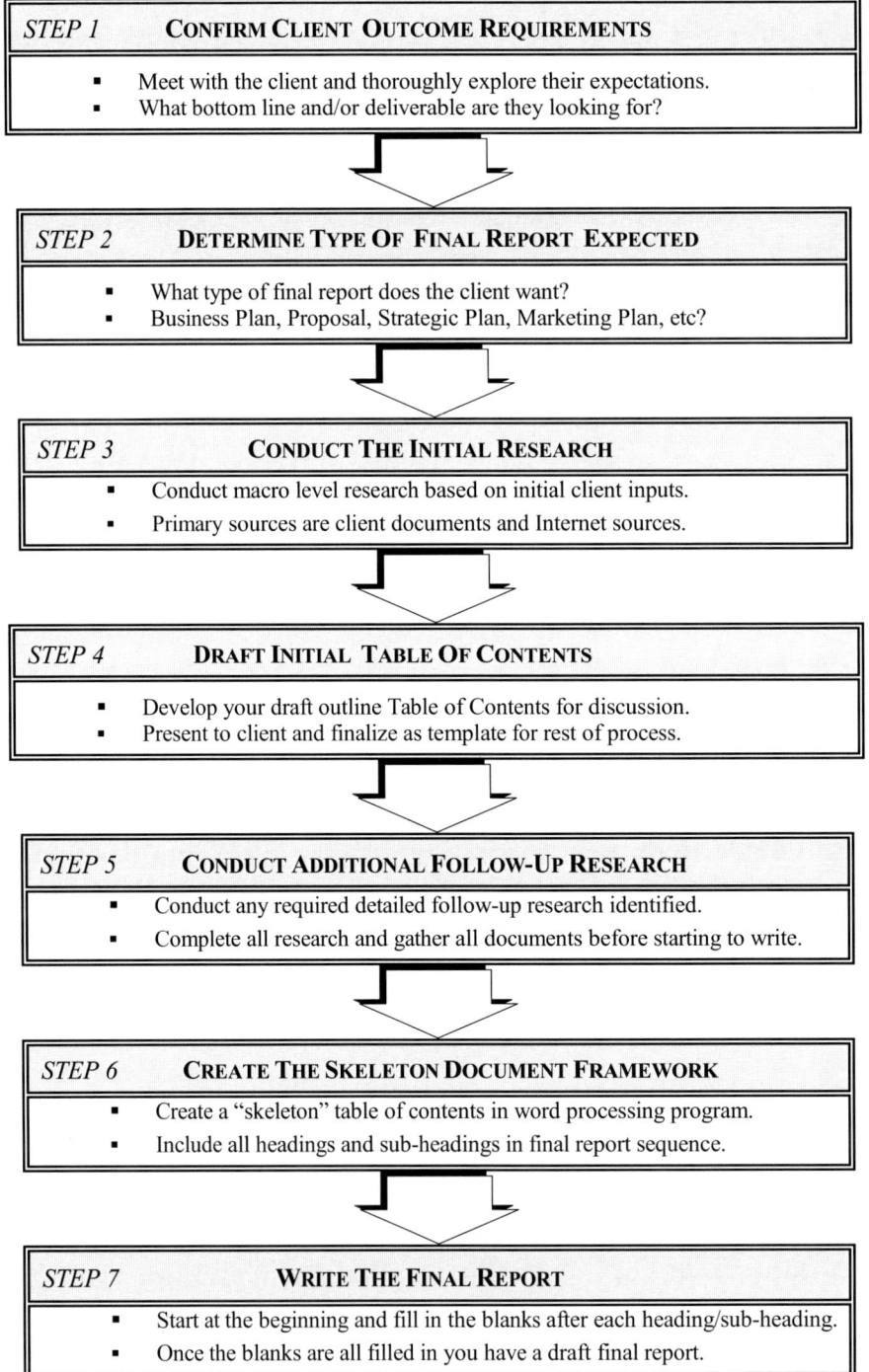

STEP 1	CONFIRM CLIENT OUTCOME REQUIREMENTS
	▪ Meet with the client and thoroughly explore their expectations. ▪ What bottom line and/or deliverable are they looking for?

STEP 2	DETERMINE TYPE OF FINAL REPORT EXPECTED
	▪ What type of final report does the client want? ▪ Business Plan, Proposal, Strategic Plan, Marketing Plan, etc?

STEP 3	CONDUCT THE INITIAL RESEARCH
	▪ Conduct macro level research based on initial client inputs. ▪ Primary sources are client documents and Internet sources.

STEP 4	DRAFT INITIAL TABLE OF CONTENTS
	▪ Develop your draft outline Table of Contents for discussion. ▪ Present to client and finalize as template for rest of process.

STEP 5	CONDUCT ADDITIONAL FOLLOW-UP RESEARCH
	▪ Conduct any required detailed follow-up research identified. ▪ Complete all research and gather all documents before starting to write.

STEP 6	CREATE THE SKELETON DOCUMENT FRAMEWORK
	▪ Create a "skeleton" table of contents in word processing program. ▪ Include all headings and sub-headings in final report sequence.

STEP 7	WRITE THE FINAL REPORT
	▪ Start at the beginning and fill in the blanks after each heading/sub-heading. ▪ Once the blanks are all filled in you have a draft final report.

These seven steps make up what I consider to be the essential process for writing ANY type of business report. Follow these steps carefully and you won't go wrong.

7 Key Steps For Writing Better Business Reports

1.   Confirm Exactly What The Client Wants

This is a very important initial step. Whether the client is you, or someone else, be sure that everyone is talking about the same thing in terms of expectations. When determining this, always think in terms of the final deliverable (usually the final report). What issues must it address? What direction/guidance is it expected to give? **What bottom line are they looking for?**

2.   Determine What Type Of Report Is Required

This is another very important matter to initially clarify. There are a number of different types of business reports. Although there is usually overlap between the different types, there are also important differences. For example, do they want: a business plan, a business proposal, a strategic plan, a corporate information management plan, a strategic business plan, a marketing plan, a financial plan, or what? **Know exactly what type of report they are expecting, from the outset.**

3.   Conduct The Initial Research

Once you know exactly what the client (or you) wants, and the type of report they are looking for, you are ready to conduct your initial pre-report research. This stage may be as simple as collecting and reading a few background documents supplied by the client, or it could involve developing questionnaires and conducting detailed interviews with the appropriate people. It will vary with each situation. **The Internet of course, can really simplify and shorten the research process; but remember to double and triple check your online sources.**

4.   Write The Table Of Contents First

In my experience, drafting the Table of Contents (TOC), before you start writing the actual report is **the single most important key** to developing a successful business report. This should be more than just a rough draft TOC. It should be a carefully thought out breakdown of exactly what you imagine the TOC will look like in the final report. Although this takes a bit of time, effort and brain power up-front, it really streamlines the rest of the process. What I do is to actually visualize the final report in my mind's eye and write the contents down. This really works! **This TOC becomes a step-by-step template for the rest of the process.**

Sidebar:

If you're writing the report for an external client, it's a good idea to present the draft Table of Contents to them at this point in the process and get their approval. This will force them to think it through and confirm what they really want at an early stage. Once they have agreed to a TOC you will have their "buy-in" for the rest of the process, therefore significantly reducing chances of any major changes or reversals at the final report phase.

5. Do Any Additional Research

After thinking through the TOC in detail, you will know if any additional research is required. If so, do this work **before you sit down and to actually write** the report. That way, once you begin the writing process you will have all of the information you need at hand and will not have to interrupt the writing process to conduct additional research.

6. Create The Skeleton Document

A trick I always use when working with MS-Word is to create a skeleton document first. That is, before I actually write any of the text I **enter the entire Table of Contents that I have already developed** into MS-Word, heading by heading, including sub-headings (see Step 4). At this point, the document is essentially a sequential series of headings and sub-headings with blank space between them. I then have MS-Word generate an automatic Table of Contents that exactly matches my planned TOC. Finally, I am then ready to start filling in the blank spaces after each heading and sub-heading in the body of the document with text.

7. Write The Report By Filling In The Blanks

That's right, at this point it's just a matter of filling in the blanks. Once the TOC skeleton framework is in place, writing the actual report becomes almost like filling in the blanks. Just start at the beginning and work your way through the headings and sub-headings, one at a time, until you get to the end. Really. At that point, **with all of the preparation done, it should be that straightforward.**

As the foregoing points clearly illustrate, the main secret to writing a successful business report is… **preparation.**

That's right… **preparation IS the secret**.

I hate to use a well-worn cliché at this point, but yes… the actual report writing process **IS as easy as filling in the blanks…**

… if, you follow the preparation steps that I recommend above.

I can't stress enough how important it is to follow the above steps in the order in which they are presented here.

Many people produce poor or marginal business reports by not doing the initial preparation properly. These people just sit down at the keyboard and start banging away, hoping that somehow it will magically all fall together into some sort of logical sequence.

It rarely works that way.

Remember, **when it comes to writing business reports it's all about the preparation.** The actual report writing is almost a secondary mechanical process.

Trust me on this one; I've "been there and done that" many times.

BUSINESS REPORT OUTLINES

Obviously I can't write the report for you here. You'll have to do that yourself.

Number one, I don't know what needs to be written.

However, I can do the next best thing. I can give you sample outline templates for the most common types of generic business reports that I have written.

This should give you a pretty good head-start.

You will at least have a clear idea as to how real business reports are structured, and what they typically contain.

In essence, with these outlines you will have your first draft of a Table of Contents for your report.

The following pages contain the actual Table of Contents from five business reports that I have written for various clients over the past few years.

1. Business Proposal
2. Corporate Profile
3. Strategic Plan
4. Project Review
5. Business Plan

For these examples, I have made a point of keeping the structure and contents of the TOC intact, exactly as they were written.

The only minor exception to this is that I have changed some identifying information such as the names of people and companies, for confidentiality reasons.

Once again, **a picture IS worth a thousand words!**

Report Outlines – Background/Context

The following brief explanations are provided to give you a little background information on each of the sample business report outlines included on the following pages to help you understand the context within which each report was written.

Business Report: Outline 1 – <u>Business Proposal</u>

This proposal was written for a consortium of major international consulting firms bidding on the first phase of a multi-million dollar airport redevelopment project. It covered the final planning phase, just prior to the full construction phase. This proposal was considered excellent and was pivotal to the consortium being chosen as the successful bidder in the competition.

Business Report: Outline 2 – <u>Corporate Profile</u>

This corporate expertise profile was developed for a major international engineering consulting company as a sort of "detailed brochure" to provide a standard/generic company profile, and to highlight its experience and capabilities related to airport development projects.

Business Report: Outline 3 – <u>Strategic Plan</u>

This corporate strategic plan is a model that I have developed over the years while doing strategic planning exercises with various companies and agencies. The Table of Contents as listed is actually a pretty good step-by-step breakdown of the actual strategic planning process.

Business Report: Outline 4 – <u>Project Review</u>

This project review and analysis report reflects a typical type of consulting assignment in which an outside consultant is called in by senior management to diagnose an ongoing project that seems to be floundering. This case involved a public agency managing a very high profile and sensitive project.

Business Report: Outline 5 – <u>Business Plan</u>

This business plan was developed for a manufacturing company that owned a leading-edge advanced technology in its industry. The main purpose of the plan was to find significant partners to help it move into the manufacturing and commercialization phases. Within four months, the company did find a major investing partner, and was working towards full commercialization.

Business Report: Outline 1 – <u>Business Proposal</u>

TABLE OF CONTENTS

Business Report: Outline 2 – <u>Corporate Profile</u>

TABLE OF CONTENTS

Business Report: Outline 3 – <u>Strategic Plan</u>

TABLE OF CONTENTS

Business Report: Outline 4 – <u>Project Review</u>

TABLE OF CONTENTS

Business Report: Outline 5 – <u>Business Plan</u>

TABLE OF CONTENTS

BUSINESS REPORT WRITING SECRETS

This section contains a few "trade secrets" that I have learned over the years when working on consulting projects that required business reports as outputs.

Let The Client "Draft" The Report For You

This refers directly to the points I was making earlier in this chapter related to the importance of "preparation". In fact, the following is the fourth point I made in "Business Report Writing Tips" at the beginning of this chapter (see page 243).

Write The Table Of Contents First

In my experience, drafting the Table of Contents (TOC), before you start writing the actual report is the single most important key to developing a successful business report. This should be more than just a rough draft TOC. It should be a carefully thought out breakdown of exactly what you imagine the TOC will look like in the final report. Although this takes a bit of time, effort and brain power up-front, it really streamlines the rest of the process. What I do is to actually visualize the final report in my mind's eye and write the contents down. This really works! **This TOC becomes a step-by-step template for the rest of the process."**

This is so important that I have actually adopted it over the years as my main strategy for dealing with clients at the very beginning of a project. Not only do I draft the Table of Contents up-front as my own guide, I also use it as an integral part of the project work plan that I present to the client in our initial meetings.

Presenting the client with a detailed report outline (i.e. Table of Contents) right at the very beginning of a project has a number of benefits as follows:

- It forces the client to think through what they really want from the project.
- It serves as an excellent vehicle for discussions about the entire project.
- It minimizes the number and degree of changes further down the line.

The following few pages illustrate exactly how I use the report Table of Contents right up-front with the client to set the agenda for the entire project. These documents are from an actual project situation that I dealt with a couple of years ago.

Project Confirmation Letter

A letter like this with a draft Table of Contents attached can be prepared after one meeting with the client.

Mr. Peter Chandler, Ph.D.
President and CEO
MicroTech Technologies Inc.
83 Ashland Place
Montreal, QC H9R 3N5

Dear Mr. Chandler:

It was nice meeting with you and Michael Lee last Friday. Further to our discussion, attached is what I propose as the structure/outline for the MicroTech Business Plan, 20xx-20xx.

Below is my estimate of the level of effort that will be involved in producing a final Business Plan based on the attached outline and using the information in the documents that you provided me with:

Task Description	Time Estimate (hrs)	Deliverables	Invoice on Delivery
Review and study all background material, develop outline of business plan, and conduct initial discussions with client.	10 to 15		
Develop first Draft of business plan for client review.	45 to 50	**Draft** Business Plan	Invoice No. 1
Discuss revisions with client, make revisions, and produce Draft Final business plan for final client review.	10 to 15	**Draft Final** Business Plan	
Produce Final version of business plan as per final client comments.	5 to 10	**Final** Business Plan	Invoice No. 2
Estimated Total	**70 to 90**		

This is my best estimate after carefully reviewing the documents you gave me. Of course, I would only bill for the actual professional time that I spend on the project. So, if it takes less time I will bill for less time. Since this is more than a standard writing job and has a business analysis component to it, the hourly rate I would normally charge would be $xxx. However, since this is our first time doing business I am reducing this rate by 10% to $xxx per hour.

The above estimate also assumes that I will produce a final electronic version of the plan for you (MS-Word), and that your company will look after all details and costs related to the production of a final hard copy report (I could look after that if required; but its cost is not included in the estimate).

If you require any additional information, please don't hesitate to contact me at (514) 998-1725.

Sincerely,

Shaun R. Fawcett, M.B.A.

Attach. (proposed report Outline)

Proposed Table of Contents

MicroTech Technologies Inc.
BUSINESS PLAN – Proposed Outline/Structure (Draft)

The above draft outline is a proposed Table of Contents for the final deliverable to the client – a Business Plan.

You can easily see the advantage of doing this thinking at the very beginning of the project:

- It achieves client buy-in at the very beginning of the project. No more final report "surprises".

- It becomes your "blueprint" for the entire project. In effect, it becomes your project work plan.

- It provides you with a very clear step-by-step template for the conduct of your research and your writing of the final report.

I used a draft version of this TOC in my meeting with the client and it allowed me to walk them through it, step-by-step, stimulating focused discussions. Based on our discussions in that meeting I made a few adjustments and the revised version of the TOC became my terms of reference for the both the project and the final report.

Use My Secret Weapon – The "UPFD"

The form in which you present your ideas, observations and/or findings in a business report is often just as important as the content that is expressed in words.

A number of years ago I was developing a report for a particularly difficult client who really needed each and every detail spelled out for him. He loved pictures and diagrams that simplified processes for him.

That's when I invented my Universal Process Flow Diagram™, or UPFD.

Well my client loved it, and so did I! Since then I've used this "secret weapon" one or more times in every business proposal or report that I have ever written. Really.

Not only does the UPFD look great; it really works!

Below are the basic components of a universal process flow diagram. It's simply a horizontal rectangle divided into two or three rows – a process heading row, followed by one or more details rows. An arrow is used to connect the boxes.

STEP 1	**REVIEW/REFINE/CONFIRM _MISSION STATEMENT_**
"The unique aim that sets the SRB apart from all others."	
■ Is the Object defined in the Act still appropriate as an overall mission?	
■ Does the Object/Mission need to be revised when Act next reviewed?	

As I mentioned above, this simple model can be easily adapted to pictorially describe just about ANY chronological or sequential process. (see page 242).

The following page contains a UPFD that I prepared to describe the process that I used in developing the Corporate Strategic Plan for one of my clients (see pages 247, 251).

In the end, I used that diagram in three different ways: as an overhead slide for presentations, in the report working papers, and in the Strategic Plan document itself. It also made a great agenda for the final strategic planning workshop!

Strategic Plan Review/Update Process

STEP 1	REVIEW/REFINE/CONFIRM *MISSION STATEMENT*

"The unique aim that sets the SRB apart from all others."

- Is the Object defined in the Act still appropriate as an overall mission?
- Does the Object/Mission need to be revised when Act next reviewed?

STEP 2	REVIEW/REVISE/UPDATE *CORE VALUES*

"The values that guide the SRB's work on an ongoing basis."

- Are the six core values identified in 1995 still appropriate and complete?
- Do additional core values need to be added to the list?

STEP 3	REVIEW/REVISE/UPDATE *SUCCESS FACTORS*

"Factors that are critical to the success of the organization."

- Is the list of factors identified in 1995 still appropriate and complete?
- Do additional success factors need to be added to the list?

STEP 4	REVIEW/REVISE/UPDATE *PUBLIC VALUE FACTORS*

"How does the SRB produce results for Canadians?"

- What specific groups and individuals does the SRB serve?
- What do these groups and individuals expect from the SRB?

STEP 5	IDENTIFY/DEFINE/PRIORITIZE *STRATEGIC ISSUES*

"Overall corporate level issues that need to be addressed."
- Identify and define all overall strategic issues that SRB should address.
- Consolidate/group/prioritize strategic issues based on pre-agreed criteria?

STEP 6	DEVELOP *STRATEGIC OBJECTIVE* STATEMENTS

"Broad statements of intent, specifying what has to be done for each issue."
- For top 10 or 12 Issues, develop statements of intent and/or outcomes.
- Develop one key overall objective statement per strategic issue.

STEP 7	IDENTIFY *PERFORMANCE INDICATORS*

"Indicators that quantify the SRB's contribution to transportation safety."
- Propose specific indicators for each of the top 10 to 12 Objectives.
- Performance indicators must be as specific and quantifiable as possible.

BUSINESS WRITING REFERENCES

Even though this guide is all about "writing business letters", as a Bonus I have included my standard quick-list of general business writing resources for your information and reference, should you need additional writing help.

There are literally thousands of business writing reference books available. The following is a "desert island" short-list of what I consider to be some of the most useful books for anyone looking for basic help in drafting their business writing projects.

WRITING STYLE REFERENCES

A Pocket Style Manual, by Diana Hacker, Bedford/St. Martin's, 5th Ed. (June 2009).
http://www.amazon.com

Basic Grammar in Use: Student's Book With Answers: Self-study Reference and Practice for Students of North American English, by Raymond Murphy with William R. Smalzer, (Sept. 2010).
http://www.amazon.com

The Chicago Manual of Style: The Essential Guide for Writers, Editors, and Publishers (16th Ed.), by Chicago Press Staff, Univ. of Chicago Press, (Aug 2010).
http://www.amazon.com

The Economist Style Guide: The Bestselling Guide To English Usage, by The Economist Books (May 2010).
http://www.amazon.com

Effective Business Writing: A Guide for Those Who Write on the Job, by Maryann V. Piotrowski, HarperCollins,2nd Revised & updated edition (March 1996).
http://www.amazon.com

The Elements of Business Writing: A Guide to Writing Clear, Concise Letters, Memos, Reports, Proposals, and Other Business Documents, by Gary Blake, Robert W. Bly, Longman; 1st edition (August 1992).
http://www.amazon.com

The Elements of Style: The Original Edition, by William Strunk (August 2009).
http://www.amazon.com

How to Say It – Third Edition: Choice Words, Phrases, Sentences & Paragraphs for Every Situation (Paperback), by Rosalie Maggio (April 2009).
http://www.amazon.com

How to Write It: A Complete Guide to Everything You'll Ever Write, by Sandra E. Lamb, (Paperback) (July 2006).
http://www.amazon.com

Merriam Webster's Collegiate Dictionary, by Merriam-Webster, Merriam Webster, 11th Edition (Hardcover, April 2008).
http://www.amazon.com

MLA Handbook for Writers of Research Papers (7th Edition) , by Joseph Gibaldi, Modern Language Association of America, (March 2009).
http://www.mla.org

Publication Manual of the American Psychological Association, Sixth Edition, American Psychological Association, (July 2009).
http://www.apa.org

Professional Writing Skills, by Janis Fisher Chan, Diane Lutovich, Advanced Communication Designs, Inc.; 2nd edition (June 1997).
http://www.amazon.com

Writers Inc.: A Student Handbook for Writing and Learning, by Patrick Sebranek, Dave Kemper, Verne Meyer, and Chris Krenzke., (Hardcover, Jan 2006).
http://www.amazon.com

Writing That Works: Communicating Effectively on the Job, by Walter E. Oliu, Charles T. Brusaw, and Gerald J. Alred (Paperback - Oct 2009).
http://www.amazon.com

WRITING HELP TOOLS AND TEMPLATES

A collection of additional writing-related resources can be found at the following links at writinghelp-central.com:

Letter Writing (personal and business)
http://www.writinghelp-central.com/letter-writing.html

Business Writing
http://www.writinghelp-central.com/business-reports.html

APA Format
http://www.writinghelp-central.com/apa.html

MLA Format
http://www.writinghelp-central.com/mla.html

In addition, my Writing Help Tools website also contains a number of other writing-related resources that may interest you:
http://www.writinghelptools.com

Instant Home Writing Kit -
How To Save Money, Time and Effort and Simplify Everyday Writing Tasks
http://instanthomewritingkit.com

Instant Business Letter Kit -
How To Write Business Letters That Get The Job Done
http://instantbusinessletterkit.com

Instant Recommendation Letter Kit -
How To Write Winning Letters of Recommendation
http://instantrecommendationletterkit.com

Instant Resignation Letter Kit -
How To Write A Super Resignation Letter and Move On With Class
http://instantresignationletterkit.com

Instant Letter Writing Kit –
How To Write Any Kind Of Letter Like A Pro
http://instantletterwritingkit.com

Instant College Admission Essay Kit -
How To Write A Personal Statement Essay That Will Get You In
http://instantcollegeadmissionessay.com

Medical Residency Personal Statement Kit -
http://www.medical-residency-statement.com

Instant Book Writing Kit -
How To Write, Publish and Market Your Own Money Making Book/eBook Online
http://instantbookwritingkit.com

How To Write A How-To Book (or eBook)
Make Money Writing About Your Favorite Hobby, Interest or Activity
http://howtowritehowto.com

ONLINE BUSINESS LETTER RESOURCES

I believe that if you faithfully follow ALL of the advice and information included in this Writing Kit you will be successful in writing virtually ANY type of business letter.

Nevertheless, even with all the information provided here, there will be some people who won't feel entirely confident until they check out every possibility and will continue to look for additional help and advice. To save those folks a lot of time and trouble I have spent many hours researching what additional online business letter writing resources are out there that one may want to consult.

In fact, there are literally tens of thousands of websites and hundreds of thousands of Web pages that contain information related to the writing of business letters.

For example, the week I researched, tested and compiled the following list I did some testing on www.google.com. When I entered the specific search phrase "write business letter", google came back with over 92,800,000 links! For the phrase "business letter writing help", over 38,200,000 relevant links were found!

So, to get that list down to a meaningful number of sites, I did a detailed review of the first 50 or so most relevant search results at both google.com and bing.com. I then chose what I considered to be the most useful, based on my assessment of quality of content. I also made a point to not include the most blatantly commercial links.

I then listed the selected sites ranked in order of their popularity according to their alexa.com traffic ratings on the day that I conducted this research. Alexa is a respected Website ranking service that computes traffic rankings by analyzing the Web usage of millions of www.alexa.com toolbar users.

Accordingly, the following section contains my researched "short-list" of the Top 20 links that I have compiled as the most useful and relevant links on the World Wide Web related to "how to write business letters".

As you can imagine, researching and compiling this short-list of links took many tedious hours, so please take advantage of the fruits of my labors.

TOP 20 BUSINESS LETTER RESOURCE LINKS

The following are what I consider to be the **Top 20 business letter writing resource and information sites on the Web.** The list was compiled to help you find any additional resources you feel you may need for help with your business letter writing.

As mentioned above, the sites are **ranked in order of popularity according to their alexa.com traffic ratings** on the day that I conducted this research.

Please Note; that at the time this research was conducted and these lists were compiled, all links were tested and were found to be in good working order.

A commercial business letter is usually used when writing from one business to ...
http://en.wikipedia.org/wiki/Business_letter

Business Letter Writing Basics... Think of a basic business letter in three steps ...
www.esl.about.com

How to Write a Business Letter... Need to write a polished, professional letter?
http://www.wikihow.com/Write-a-Business-Letter

Writing the Basic Business Letter... Purdue Online Writing Lab...
http://owl.english.purdue.edu/owl/resource/653/01/

Writer's Handbook for Business Letters... instructional materials we've developed.
http://www.writing.wisc.edu/Handbook/BusinessLetter.html

Business letters are formal letters... They could be about many different subjects...
http://auspost.com.au/education/letterwriting/students/business-letters.html

Professional English writing... business letters, business e-mails...
http://www.englishtown.com/community/portal/business/bizwrite/free.aspx

Business Letter Writing Center... help writing business letters for many situations...
http://writingcenter.unc.edu/handouts/business-letters/

How To Write A Business Letter… Writing a business letter isn't complicated…
http://business.lovetoknow.com/wiki/How_To_Write_A_Business_Letter

Help with formal and business letter writing… A summary of writing rules…
http://www.usingenglish.com/resources/letter-writing.php

Business English Letters… Most professional people have to write business letters...
http://www.englishclub.com/business-english/business-letters.htm

The CSU Writing Studio Guides… to Writing Business Letters…
http://writing.colostate.edu/guides/guide.cfm?guideid=71

Business English Phrases… useful phrases and vocabulary for writing business letters.
http://www.learn-english-today.com/business-english/business-letters.html

How to Write a Business Letter…Sample and Tips…
http://www.eduers.com/businessletter/index.html

Letter Writing & Sample Letters... Letter Writing Guide contains tips, advice…
www.**letterwriting**guide.com/

Lesson 29: Business letter is a formal communication between people or companies…
http://www.studyenglishtoday.net/writing-business-letters.html

How to Write a Business Letter…
http://www.write101.com/businessletter.htm

How to write a business letter... Each year I see thousands of letters…
http://www.cyberbee.com/science/buslet.html

Business Letter Writing Services… If you need any kind of business letter…
http://www.clear-writing.com/letter-writing-services.html

Top 10 Tips … For Writing Business Letters…
http://www.penmachine.com/topten.html

INDEX

A

acceptance letter, 124

address block, 44

alexa.com, 265, 266

amazon.com, 9, 261, 262

announcement – new location, 142, 187

announcement letter, 32

annual report, 71, 75, 76, 144

apology letters, 32, 72, 129, 142, 187

attention line, 33, 34

award nomination, 71, 79, 80

B

background information, 197, 198, 211, 229

back order notice, 142, 171

barnesandnoble.com, 9

basic-block style, 38, 39

body block, 33, 35

brother, 198, 233

business associate/colleague, 72, 103, 145, 198, 223

business envelope format, 44

business memorandum (memo), 49

business plan, 123, 242, 246, 247, 253, 255, 257

business proposal, 72, 129, 131, 246-248

business report, 10, 15, 241-247, 254, 258

business writing, 261

business-to-business letters, 7, 9, 14, 30, 31, 129, 237

business-to-customer letters, 7, 9, 14, 31, 187

C

cancellation notice, 197, 211

carbon copy, 36

closing salutation, 45

collection letters, 95, 96, 153-157

commendation letters, 71-81, 129, 132, 136, 170

company information, 141, 143

complaint letters, 72, 129, 133

complaint response, 141, 147

complimentary closing, 33, 35

condolence letters, 71, 79, 82, 142, 187, 190, 198, 233, 234

congratulations letters, 31, 73, 129

consulting services, 124

consumer show, 72, 109

continuation page format, 44

contract letters, 197, 211, 214-216

corporate profile, 246, 247, 250

corporate style manual, 51

cover/covering letters, 31, 32, 54, 75-78, 119, 125, 143-146, 165, 182, 198, 237

credit approval, 71, 95, 97, 141, 157

credit denial, 141, 157

credit letter, 32

credit program solicitation, 71, 95, 99

credit refusal, 71, 95, 98

customer appreciation, 149, 198, 237

customer relations letter, 32, 147

customer service, 133

D

date line, 33, 34, 39

delayed order notice, 142, 171

delinquency notice, 141

downloadable templates, 17, 22

downsizing, 71, 79, 90

E

employee letters, 31, 71, 79, 197, 199
enclosure/attachment line, 33, 36
exclusive member mailing, 142, 179
expedite payment, 197, 211, 214

F

family, 180, 191, 198, 200, 233
fill-in-the-blank, 9, 17, 18, 19, 23
financial hardship letters, 198, 229-232
financial letters, 31, 32, 95
follow-up letters, 141, 142, 147
font style, 45
formatting guidelines, 9, 45
former employee, 72, 103, 142, 187
franchise application, 141, 143, 145
full-block style, 38, 41, 51
fully-formatted, 8, 9, 17, 21, 22, 71, 141
fundraising letters, 142, 187

G

goodbye letters, 197, 199, 205
grammar, 261

H

holiday season wishes, 71, 79, 83
home-based business, 10

I

industry mail-out, 72
interrupted service notice, 141, 147
introduction letters, 13, 31, 32, 69, 103, 167
invitation letters, 31, 73, 129
invoices, 72, 95, 141, 157

J

job reference, 71, 79
justification letter, 73

L

leave-behind letter, 142, 179
legal documents, 71, 75
letter of acknowledgement, 141, 147
letter generators, 23
letter of commendation, 197, 199, 204
letter of credit, 72, 95, 101, 197, 211, 213
letter of interest, 119, 120, 197, 211, 212
letter of introduction, 12, 13, 103, 167
letter of reference, 197, 199, 224
letterhead block, 33, 34, 45
letter of transmittal, 143
letter-writing tips, 9, 263
level of service, 133
line-spacing, 47, 48

M

marketing and promotion, 197, 219-222
marketing letter, 31, 32, 179
meeting follow-up, 72, 109
memo, 49, 51, 79, 80, 93, 94, 199
moving instructions, 71, 79, 85

N

new loans manager, 141, 167
new program, 197, 219
new service available, 141, 167
new service representative, 141, 167
news release, 72, 109, 110, 115
notice of audit, 197, 211

O

order-related letters, 142, 171
order-status letter, 32
organization change, 71, 79, 86
organizations, 49, 51, 71, 121, 140

Printed by BoD™in Norderstedt, Germany

9 780981 289885